The Surviving Solo Series

Back On The Shelf

Mary Hadow

BACK ON THE SHELF

Other Titles by Mary Hadow:

Surviving Solo Vol 1: Dare B&B

Surviving Solo Vol 3: Moving On By Staying Still

Snow Way

Copyright © 2017 Mary Hadow

All rights reserved.

BACK ON THE SHELF

To Ange, Marsha, Lise and Joolie Poolie
for your ongoing interest and encouragement in all things Mary

BACK ON THE SHELF

CONTENTS

1	Got The T-Shirt	Pg 9
2	Single Life on Dartmoor	Pg 25
3	Getting Nowhere, Slowly	Pg 71
4	Will It Never End?	Pg 107
5	More of the Same	Pg 157
6	Love In the Country	Pg 203

BACK ON THE SHELF

First Date

He laughs out loud in his car,
As he drives on through the storm.
Who lives in the middle of nowhere?!
The girl with the blonde hair and the big blue eyes,
The girl with the beautiful smile.

His heart soars and his tummy flips
As he drives fast across the moor.
What will she really be like?
This mystery online date,
He stumbled upon just a week ago today.

He pulls up into her drive
And takes a very deep breath.
First he is greeted by a friendly dog
Then she is walking slowly towards him.
She smiles and the butterflies melt away.

Seven hours later the date is now coming to a close.
He had found it hard to tear himself away from her.
The day had gone as well as it could, he thinks,
But how happy would he have been at the end
With a stolen kiss, to take with him, on his way?

She seemed quite sure of herself and so honest
Yet also quite cautious and so guarded?
He wished he knew how she truly felt.
He would have to tread carefully here,
Though caution favours the brave, they say.

He laughed on his drive home as well,
As he remembered all her stories.
The sun was even shining over the moor now!
He cannot wait to see her again,
This girl with the beautiful smile.

Ben, June 2017

BACK ON THE SHELF

1 GOT THE T-SHIRT

Dating Sites For Total Losers
05/01/2014

"Public School/University 5'9" bubbly blonde (26) believes all unattached entertaining men (28-40) are in hiding. Please prove her wrong. Fulham."

My first ever lonely hearts ad. Placed in 'Private Eye' in 1986. It cost £21.

Three of my best friends and I were all on the shelf - but they were prettier, nicer and more charming, so I swallowed my pride (the 'personals' were even more taboo back then) and came up with this idea to steal a march on them.

Later on, Nicholas Coleridge, now God of All Magazines Throughout The Universe And Beyond, but then an old school chum and editor of Harpers & Queen, commissioned me to write an article about the people I met, which proved to be remarkably enthusiastically received. Perhaps because it was illustrated with a photo of me dressed in a sharp purple suit, leaning against the willy of a naked stone statue with its arms and legs missing.

The pic was taken by society photographer, John Swannell, who kept yelling at me: "Relax!" Entirely calculated to have the opposite effect - rather like riding teachers!

My ad generated lots of replies, but disappointingly none of them proved me wrong.

Unfazed, I took up graphology - the interpretation of handwriting - so that another time I would be able to choose better from the scores of written responses I received.

Three years later, and with the country's first Distinction in a Graphology Diploma under my belt, I found myself using my new skill professionally, helping in recruitment, and writing articles for the national media about celebrities varying from Michael Jackson to serial killer Nurse Alitt. But that's another story.

Finding that perfect man continued to elude me. Until I bumped into my now ex-husband in the crypt of St Mary's Church, Battersea, at my cousin's 30th birthday party.

Twenty-five years later, husband history (not quite so perfect after all), and with the invention of the internet, how things have changed! No need for laborious hand-written missives anymore. I can chuck my Diploma on the fire!

And yet. How good actually is this online dating stuff?

Recently, I came across an article in the 'Daily Mail' called "All Dating Sites are for Total Losers".

So that would be nine million of us, according to their stats. Wow!

Their writer bases her thesis on personal first hand experience of just three encounters.

Whereas, only the other day, Chris Evans told us on Radio 2 that his chum had finally found love after meeting over 70 dates!

The Daily Mail tells us that 'bald, white bearded, broke, fat, dull, over-50s men' are expecting to find themselves an 'affluent, beautiful, young, free housekeeper.'

Well it strikes me that the lady in question's three dates might have found her 'smug, complacent, arrogant, opinionated, impatient, judgmental and generally up her own arse'. Also possibly 'fat-ist, beard-ist, hair-ist, age-ist, and money-ist'.

Added to which, I bet she's over fifty, with bat-wings, a floppy fat tummy, saggy large bum, cellulite thighs; criss-crossed wrinkles over her chest and neck; and no doubt the moles on her face are starting to sprout hair. She probably also suffers hormonal mood swings, and wakes up at night in bed sweating.

Just like me! No wonder I'm struggling a bit. She sounds good fun!

LoveLife - Lack Of
15/04/2014

I just got dumped.

By email.

After what has been a three month, sort-of, relationship.

He had turned up on Encounters – the website for readers of The Times and The Telegraph, and devotees of Classic FM – only thirty minutes after I finally decided to sign up on it again, having just finished a rather special relationship with a very nice chap called Malcolm, whom I had met via Guardian Soulmates three years previously. This new bloke was so clearly the perfect man for me, I wanted to shout "I love him!" from a mountain top!

But it all turned out to be rather a non-event. His monster ex-wife was causing him daily panic-attacks, as he attempted to provide some stability and routine for his autistic youngest son.

Really though. To get chucked by email. How rude.

So I rang him up and told him so.

And now I'm back on the faithful old Encounters Dating Website again.

Maybe I'll give Guardian Soulmates a go too. It's possible the people on that are more interesting and quirky than Encounters subscribers. The only trouble is that they probably like reading The Guardian. The minute they hear I buy the Daily Mail for its coverage of 'Britain's Got Talent' (the whole of Page 3 was devoted to a performing Eagle Owl yesterday), they'll run in the opposite direction.

In my opinion, people who buy The Guardian (or that oddly named leftie publication 'The Independent' for that matter) are far more bigoted than Mail readers. Unlike them, Mail readers don't believe everything we read in our paper. Do we actually even read it? Or just look at the pictures?

I am a Woman Of Substance. I have a beautiful large home, my own thriving business, financial security, two well-balanced (at the moment anyway) children at private school, land, loads of friends, functional loving family, reasonably cordial relationship with Ex, hardly any baggage, hardly any bitterness, I'm mobile with some free time on my hands, I am tall, fit, good looking (I hope so anyway, can't really tell), friendly, funny and independent.

If I were a man on any dating site, I would be eaten alive. It's just not fair. Perhaps it would be better if only I came across as a little more vulnerable.

Zoe Ball has just played a song on Radio 2 called "I'm coming back as a Man". I'm off to download it onto my iPod.

Vicarious Love
15/04/2014

"If you write about me on that blog of yours, I'll never speak to you again," warns my friend Stephen. As it happens, Stephen is, after all, still speaking to me, because that is not his real name, so he'll never know it's him. Ha ha!

I have to be careful what I put on the blog, though - I mean absolutely anybody could be reading it!

To try and keep censoring myself, I tend to imagine my Mum perching on my shoulder, telling me off; or Uncle Jock, ex-army and CEO of the AA, who once thundered at me: "I can't think why you want to tell the whole world about your sex-life!" after my Harpers & Queen piece was published.

The thing is, of course, that I don't want guests of the B&B business that I run from my home, to think that they're going to be written about, and therefore not want to come to stay. And the same goes for friends and potential suitors.

But I can't help writing today. Because I have just realised that I am living vicariously off other people's love.

My B&B, Wydemeet, in remostest Dartmoor, is a house of love. 99% of people who stay come as a couple.

We've had our first engagement here, by the stepping stones; we've had couples who've been married 40+ years; couples celebrating wedding anniversaries; and now we have a young pair on their 'MiniMoon', who got married on Saturday, which, much to her delight, was my daughter Faye's twelfth birthday.

I would want to come to Wydemeet if I were loved up. It's terribly romantic, the rooms are spacious, soft and comfortable; you can sit in a hot tub together under the stars; or lounge around in front of the log fire in the cosy sitting room; you have breakfast side by side, in your pyjamas if you want, looking out at the trees in the garden outside; you can go back to your room for the rest of the day if you like; the walks along the rivers and across the moors are private and spectacular.

It's all a bit like Steve Wright's Radio 2 Sunday Love Songs programme - watching my guests gives me faith that deep love and affection still exist in spades.

Weirdos
16/04/2014

"Only VERY bossy ladies please" requests 'Totdevoted' on Encounters. I immediately sign him up as one of my 'favourites', and he returns the favour.

I scroll down to find out more about him.

"I work in the City and I am smart, successful and driven at work," he says. "I am well-travelled and very well educated, cultured and well-read. I am seeking a long term relationship and REAL commitment - so no flings please." How exciting!

Skipping a bit, I get to, "I seek the kind of woman who demands worship and pampering and obedience from her man." FANTASTIC! blah blah "I do hope this piques your interest - if you understand how a man can adore worship and obey his diva Goddess... " errrrrr

For his ideal match: "I mean REALLY bossy and demanding."

"Body type: A few extra pounds; Curvaceous; Full figured."

I consider messaging back saying "I'm afraid I'm too thin." But it's just all too weird.

I don't know whether this internet dating stuff is evil, or a force for real good. Both I suppose.

What I do know is that it is extremely time-consuming, addictive and brutal.

Even if you've ceased subscribing, the agents keep your details up online, unless you ask them not to, and every couple of days send you a selection of 'matches', who are usually short, fat, bald, broke, and live at least 100 miles away. Just as the Daily Mail journalist discovered.

I am constantly experimenting with the thing - you can check out who has looked at your 'profile'; and there's a 'Top 20' on the Encounters site, featuring the most 'favourited' or 'messaged' people on the site. The women look gorgeous and young, and their photos look professionally posed and airbrushed (unlike mine); while the men are mostly hideous. Some people 'favourite' everyone they can, hoping to get 'favourited' back again and thus into the Top 20. I haven't tried this yet but could be tempted...

I don't think many people are deliberately dishonest, but some of my pics are nearly five years old simply because nobody's taken any of me recently - not because I was nearly two stone lighter in those days!

Moist
30/04/2014

Encounters has gone mental!

"Wot a Kisser!" my friend Judith emailed me excitedly the other day. She is also signed up, as is every single single person I know.

She is so thrilled by her own result, after months of nothing happening, that when I went to stay with her last week, after a bottle of red wine she started 'messaging' about 1,000 people (including one or two girls) on my behalf, whom I would never have dreamed of contacting myself.

Eg, she contacted lots of good looking men from the Top 20 who live miles away and will already be receiving 200 messages daily; and then a whole load of people simply because the site informed us that they were logged in at the time.

The next day I was inundated with replies. Despite the fact that Judith's computer hadn't worked properly, so the funny, charming, loving messages she had sent out had been turned into gobbledegook.

So since then I have been very busy practising my amateur writing skills, bantering, if there is such a verb, with all my new admirers dotted around the country.

My favourite is a journalist who lives in an eco-house near 'Chippers' (Chipping Norton), who says he is game to play footsie at Faye's Prep School Quiz Night next week. He is a motoring correspondent and is going to drive me there in the latest Maserati (he is not Jezza Clarkson, fortunately, or unfortunately).

We'll believe all that in the unlikely event of it ever happening. His writing skills are such that, even without a picture, at one stage he made it to Number 2 in the Encounters Most Popular List. I am very impressed, as I have yet to make it onto the List at all.

Anyway, he has challenged me to use the word 'moist' in my next blog. So I have. Moist.

Be Careful Who You Meet!
06/05/2014

A transgender hip replacement surgeon was the first person Mr Dumped-Me-By-Email and I realised that we both knew in common. The surgeon's name used to be John, and now it is Jennifer. My sister, who was operated on by him/her, did comment that Jennifer looked a bit 'manly'.

Strongest man in the world, also ex-president of the Budgerigar Society, Geoff Capes, turns out to be the mutual point of contact between my new journalist friend and me. I once employed Capes to judge a "Bravest Little Boy" competition when I was doing PR for Tonka Trucks. Cape wouldn't do anything I asked, so I had to issue instructions via my photographer who was a bloke.

My three year Guardian Soulmates date, Malcolm, discovered that we had attended the same skating party in Suffolk when I was six.

And now my Nemesis, 'She', not content with pinching my husband, has recently moved on to Malcolm's first cousin, who just so happens to be a Duke. I wish She would stop following me around!

Another blind date I was recently set up with remembered meeting someone like me 30 years ago, at a party full of Exeter University undergraduates. He arranged to see her the following day, but he arrived four hours late, and missed her. It turned out that that person was me. He drove a Ferrari at the time, and had a pet parrot too. Oh what could have been!

Who's Brainier?
10/05/2014

Frederic Chopin wrote the "Minute Waltz". I know the piece quite well, because I've timed myself playing it. I take five minutes to get through it (including repeats) so if you try waltzing along to me at the piano, you will fall over.

"Who wrote the Minute Waltz?" was the only question (out of 166) that I could answer last night, at Faye's School Quiz.

Normally I win quiz nights by identifying the cleverest people in the room and buying them drinks; but last night my team "Snowflakes Plus", comprising the school ski trip, came sixth out of seven.

Ever since studying graphology, I have been particularly interested in different kinds of intelligence. Graphologists tend to look at four: memory retention, practical, intuitive, and planning/manipulative.

Once upon a time I would have felt highly inadequate after an evening like last night's. Even though we only came sixth, I still thought that every member of our team was intellectually electric! I was stunned by their Encyclopaedic brains!

But I did wonder if any of them would manage to run a successful B&B like mine.

Sadly my Maserati-driving journo failed to materialise.

Don't Get Divorced!
10/06/2014

Just don't get divorced if you can possibly help it! The grass isn't greener!

Go through your Christmas card list. How many 'happily married' couples' lives are you jealous of? Nobody's probably.

Whatever happens, if you get divorced, you will be poorer. And you will make your children cry. And you will never truly enjoy Christmas again.

We have such a lovely time when Ex comes to see Faye, often picking up our son Will (16) from boarding school on the way.

Steak, ducks legs, macaroni cheese. Yesterday I cooked everybody's favourite things for lunch. And then we set off on the 'Man vs Horse vs Bicycle' race, to Princetown.

Man - ie Ex; won. Verdict: easily.

Bicycle (Will) - last, by half-an-hour, having just avoided getting electrocuted in a lightning storm.

And then after all the fun, everybody had to go back home in their different directions. All suddenly seems very quiet, I'm back to being me all alone.

Meanwhile, my romantic life isn't going very well.

At the moment, there's a lovely, good-looking, tall bloke from Encounters, called Peter, who drives a small sports car, and has taken me out for fantastic lunches twice, who understands a wine list, and who pays.

That is a most exciting start, but he doesn't want a relationship.

Then there's someone from Taunton who writes so well that I've paid £14 to join matches.com in order to be in contact with him.

And then there's my last, final, forlorn and expensive hope - I've booked a Nielson sailing beach resort holiday in Turkey for Will, Faye and myself. A week in July, when I may bump into the solvent single Dad of my dreams! But that will only happen if our passports get back in time. I might have to contact our local MP.

Back to (slimming) Black
10/06/2014

The upside of getting the heave-ho is that you lose weight.

The Jilted Wives Club, comprising Loelia, Juliette and me, lost six stone between us, shortly after the departure of our husbands.

Juliette, in her miniscule hot-pants, soon pulled a blind man in Costa's, and then a little later, two men who could see, so who could properly appreciate her pert bum.

Loelia was repeatedly hooted at by lorry drivers on the A30, as we chatted outside Launceston's Spud-U-Like. Her Elle MacPherson giraffe-legs encased in skin-tight jeans and long boots, and her thick, brunette Kate Middleton hair waving in their slipstream could not be ignored. My son Will awarded Loelia the 'fittest mum in the school' award.

Meanwhile, immersed in my diet of misery, fags and frozen-platters-for-one, I initially found keeping the weight off quite easy, and for the first time discovered myself branching out into coloured clothing!

But now I am back to black. The post-break-up slimmed-down version of me, five years on, is fast disappearing, and soon I will be back to normal, dammit.

Fashion Tips for the Maturer Man
10/06/2014

Experience of meeting various online dates makes me think there's a danger for you men, if you're out of circulation for too long and have had no woman to look after/nag you, that you forget how to dress. Or how to stay properly clean. And a tendency to overlook where your hair now is and isn't growing.

Call me shallow, but on a blind date first impressions are critical. Perhaps you think that love should conquer all - whatever you look, smell or feel like - but I think this attitude will leave you disappointed.

It's worth remembering that like you, we middle-aged women are also trying to get our eye back in, and learn to fancy middle-aged people with crepey necks, thin grey hair, paunches and bad backs. The last time we were all on the market everybody was in their twenties and thirties!

Straightforward proof for women that we no longer look as we once did comes when we pass a building site. The silence is even worse than the wolf whistles used to be.

Anyhow. I think it's still worth bothering so I've put together a little guide for blokes - of what I think is important anyway, moving down the body from the top of your head to the tips of your toes:

HAIR (or lack of it) ON YOUR HEAD
Long hair dark - good; long hair grey - bad.
Bald with straggly sides? Give me strength.
Comb-overs – like limp handshakes.
Regular haircuts are more important than ever for old blokes.

FACE
Eyebrows, nose hair, ear hair, toe hair needs to be regularly trimmed or you'll look like an old tramp, or Dennis Healey. Those trimmer gadgets make great stocking fillers!
Contacts or a laser operation – lose years!
Lightweight specs frames if you must, unless your face is so ugly it needs covering up.
A big no to light-reactive specs' lenses – we'll think you're blind rather than cool, when they stay dark as the clouds gather - or when you're

indoors.
Brown/black stubble - tick. Silver/grey stubble - cross.
Just because you can now grow hair more easily on your chin than on the top of your head doesn't mean that you should!

BODY
Choose your look, not a combination. Country caszh? Town caszh? Nautical, beachy, sporty, dinner party; but not all at once. A fleece, lambswool sweater, floppy linen trousers and leather boots all together? Non.
Tuck in all shirts - the 'vertical hang' from even the tiniest paunch does few favours, and, presumably, is also draughty. Beware of floppy old fleeces and jumpers that might further draw attention to this problem.
No thick shirts under thin jumpers.
White polo neck jumpers are verboten, unless you're in the Alps in winter and you're thin.
Now that you're old, creased clothes make you look like an old tramp rather than a young hippy.
Thick woolly jumpers make you look fat.
No anoraks unless they're Musto.

LOWER HALF
Tailored and fitted looks better on saggy old bumpy bodies than floppy trousers or combats which are designed for young surfers without excess flesh and skin.
Hurray! None of us is old enough for elasticated waistbands yet!
Are your trousers long enough?
Open toed shoes are a challenge, now our toenails are becoming thick and yellow. Women's advantage is that we can cover them with Shellac.
Flip-flops, provided they come complete with the bit that goes between your toes could be OK.
Sandals with socks – nooooooooooooooooooooooooo!
Trainers (unless you're going to the gym) noooooooo! They're for people with arthritis. Bright white trainers? Any white shoes at all? AAGGGHH!
Thick crepe soles – avoid!
Long, thin wellies – yummy! Short, wide ones – yuck!
Skinny swimming trunks? Erm OK – but only for Daniel Craig or Tom Daley.

SMELL

I've received a couple of reports from women dating onliners of men who live singly smelling 'musty'. Really. Well. No one can kiss someone new who actually smells 'old'. Wash your rarely worn clothes and air your cloakroom and coats.
Make sure your home doesn't smell of cat.
BO might be OK on Venice Beach, but it's horrid on Old Bloke.
Clean your teeth twice a day, and floss, or use those stick-things, if you don't want your gums to recede even more quickly than they already are.

I've found that charity shops aren't bad if you're a bit broke after the divorce. I've just returned from Newton Abbot with two lambswool jumpers and a Saville Row morning suit for smart weddings, all for £25. I'll sell the morning suit on eBay for a profit if nobody I know wants it.

And now I've just checked the internet for a similar list of do's and don'ts for dressing the older man. Oh dear. There's a site hosted by some ghastly white-haired American moron with a beard, wearing a stupid jacket and tie, who says the exact opposite of what I've listed above.

How Honest A Friend?
10/06/2014

I seem to have gone a bit 'lookist' recently - or perhaps this is a permanent state of mind. You certainly wouldn't believe it to look at me, for all the time it might appear that I devote to the subject.

Last Monday, I leaped out of bed, threw on a few clothes, and rushed downstairs to prepare Faye's pony for her, just in time for her to join Neighbour for a short ride.

As we went out of the gate together, me in a vest, no bra, a fleece, some jodhpurs and no knickers; my hair matted, and what was left of yesterday's mascara and eyeliner smeared down the sides of my face reaching to my chin, Faye casually commented, "You look better without make-up."

A conclusion that I had been slowly moving towards on my own. But why? Make-up is designed to improve your looks, not make you look worse.

I think this is a touchy, sensitive, intensely personal subject.

Should you, for instance, tell your best friend that her teeth are yellowing and need bleaching, her heavy green eyeshadow makes her look like a 70s retro, her eye-liner and mascara are all blotchy, her foundation is much too thick and exaggerating her open pores and wrinkles, her haircut does her face-shape no favours, the colour she's chosen for it makes her look older than if she just left the grey streaks in, and that the clothes she's wearing make her look fatter than she is underneath?

I think that commenting on this kind of thing is helpful, and the mark of brave, real friendship - if it's true, and she can do something about it. Especially as we all get older and our eyesight worsens, so we can't see ourselves very well in the mirror anymore.

I had been trying to emulate all those young people with apparently flawless matt skin, who embrace the use of these new kinds of foundation that didn't exist in my day. I've also borrowed some really black eyeliner from my great friend Annabelle who works in the city in central London.

But Faye is correct. It all just looks wrong, wrong, wrong in the back of beyond in Dartmoor, so I am returning to tinted moisturiser, a bit of mascara, and chapstick as a cheap and natural-looking alternative to lipstick. Thank you, Faye! You are my true friend.

BACK ON THE SHELF

2 SINGLE LIFE ON DARTMOOR

The 24 Hour Rule
16/06/2014

Last week, two Mums had a bitch-fight in the car park of Faye's smart school.

Well not quite precisely that.

Actually, they shouted at each other, and then one of them cried and called the other a nasty name.

I was sad because I know both of them and they are both nice. And they each had their point, but the environment was not conducive to rational thought or discussion, as we all stood out in the rain and wind, waiting for a summit meeting in which to discuss the school's future.

With around 100 pupils, Faye's school achieves places, and even scholarships, for children going to Eton, Harrow and Winchester. A mad proportion of them end up doing Oxbridge. Every year its children win academic, music, art and all-rounder scholarships worth £100,000s to all the best schools in the South West. This year, so far, 13 pupils have won a total of 16 scholarships, and the entire top year group has passed Common Entrance.

Over the last six months, just some of the highlights include this anonymous, sweet little school, *winning* the *national* prep schools' Rugby 7s at Oundle; winning a national IAPS team trampolining competition in

Croydon; and best school in all three age-groups and both genders of the Devon and Cornwall athletics championships. It has county players in hockey and cricket, national diving champions, and it came 6th in the U14s national schools show-jumping in Buckinghamshire, two of its four team members, on their titchy ponies, aged just eight.

Yet, like so many other rural prep schools, its numbers have halved over the past few years, and the governors have told us that we are to merge with the less expensive, less successful, less beautiful school across the river, which isn't geared towards its leavers going on to posh boarding schools. There are simply not enough children in the area to fill up both.

Feelings are running high.

One family is so rich, and has so many children to educate, that it wants to buy the school outright.

Some of the unsolicited emails I'm being sent are extraordinarily vitriolic. If their authors had gone through a divorce, they would have learned the 24 hour rule. Never press 'send' til you've read the thing again a day later.

I am sooooooooooo tempted to get involved in the scrapping!

Life After Divorce
22/06/2014

Last week I spotted a small sign outside a nearby farmer's gate saying 'Barn Dance'. On the other side of the notice it said 'Open to All', June 21st. That was the Summer Solstice - yesterday - for anyone who didn't notice how long the day lasted.

So I was faintly appalled that I knew nothing about it, and was not aware of anyone I knew going to it. No one had mentioned it to me, yet it was obviously going to be a big night, right in my hamlet.

Neighbour, bringing round her delicious eggs for my B&Bers, clearly was aware of it, though. Apparently the evening had been organised to raise funds for my children's old village primary school.

In my loneliness, I think I'm becoming a bit of a pariah around here. It must look a bit odd - this woman keeping going, running an unnecessarily large house in the middle of nowhere, alone with just her young daughter home at weekends, for company.

I don't really care if people think I'm Mad Mary of the Moor, but I do find it hard to attend these social gatherings full of indigenous local people - all of whom have partners, most of whom are related to each other, and with whom, generally speaking, I have so little in common.

I've been here nearly twenty years now, but I'm not part of the soil. Not even rural really - I still don't know the names of the fields, tors nor birds.
I prefer walking in a flowery swimming costume, silk sarong and sparkly flip-flops, than in heavy walking boots and thick socks, wielding those silly sticks. The main reason I have horses is so that I can sit down going uphill.

Faye didn't really want to go to the dance either. She hasn't seen her local friends since last year at Widecombe Fair, when they sweetly came up to say hello, and she rushed off to the dog show, looking and sounding like an unfriendly, arrogant, posh girl, when in fact she was just suffering from an eleven-year-old shy-on.

But we made ourselves go, and I am so glad that we did. I would have been devastated to have only heard about it afterwards.

This part of Dartmoor still holds events which take you back 100 years.

For instance, every year there's a cricket match, which to me seems a bit like the Henley of Dartmoor. It's held in the most beautiful natural amphitheatre with views right across to the sea; the first match of the day is played by women and children, and the second by men. Everyone comes dressed in whites, and they bring marquees, gazebos, tables and chairs, and ice buckets, BBQs and even hammocks!

Sometimes it's rather dangerous. One year Ex hit heads with a jockey while fielding, got severely concussed and ended up in hospital. There was something he was desperate to tell me as they took him away in the ambulance. He remembered what it was later - that he'd been having an affair with my friend for two years and was leaving me. But that's another story...

The Dance last night was held in a large field and huge barn. The field was freshly mown, and, lit by the fading evening sunlight, were a bucking bronco and several bouncy castles for a vast crowd of shrieking local children.

The barn itself was immaculate - about 100 metres long, featuring local jazz, soul, blues and rock bands, and even little kiddies playing and singing to us all.

The young were everywhere, and almost everyone I've met in my twenty moorland years was there.

After a shaky start, and a little word in a few little girls' ears from me, Faye ended the evening happily sitting in the family car of her erstwhile best friend from their alma mater, making elastic bands into funny shapes. It was as if they had never been separated.

We were part of the most perfect evening imaginable.

Being Virgo
23/06/2014

I've realised why I appear to myself, and probably everybody else, to be so obsessed with this internet dating thing. It's because I'm a Virgo, and I just can't rest until I've properly completed the job in hand, whatever it is, to the best of my ability.

Which, as it happens, I've just arranged.

I have now got profiles up on three sites: Encounters, Guardian Soulmates, and match.com; and can't do much more. I've told my various audiences exactly who I am, whom I would like to meet, and then made up a sort of TripAdvisor Review about myself, written by a fictitious first date. I think all internet dating sites should carry reviews, in the same way as hotel sites do. I've given myself five blobs, naturally, and described myself as 'an extremely attractive woman'.

I wonder if it will work?

Nothing else has, so I can't lose. The trouble is, looking at all the men available on the sites, I'm not sure if I'd want any of them anyway.

Poison
02/07/2014

This morning I looked like one of those characters in a cartoon where water streams out of its eyes in a gush.

I don't remember ever crying so hard - not ever. Except for the time that our first dog died, when I was seven.

Last month I poisoned Twiglet, our wonder-dog, by giving him an ibuprofen after Neighbour's dogs ripped his leg open. £450, a Sunday overnight drip, hundreds of pills and four weeks later, he is now as good as new, no thanks to me.

Today I poisoned my horse. With rat poison.

She was crashing around the stable, dripping all over with sweat, lip curling, rolling on her sides, scraping her front hooves on the concrete, gasping.

In a way I am relieved that I can still feel at all, and so hard. I was beginning to think that I had become a bit emotionless, but clearly it's all still there, latent. I don't know how actors can portray that amount of sheer grief unless they have felt it themselves, and it's taken me til I'm 54.

I rang the vet four times: "Hurry hurry hurry hurry" I sobbed. I got the picnic stool out and sat near adorable Vegas, whispering "I'm so sorry," to her, over and over and over again and stroking her sweat-drenched neck.

Gradually she quietened. I wondered whether she would shortly lie down and die.

After an hour I heard Vivian the vet's car finally arriving, and Vivian came in and took Vegas' heartbeat and listened to her gut.

"Clinically she's perfectly OK," she said cheerfully.

Vegas had barged through a side-door into a small section of the barn which had two small trays of rat poison on the ground, and had clearly panicked as she couldn't turn around to get out again. She must have eventually backed out in fright.

On close inspection we found it difficult to believe my horse had actually eaten any of the poison - it didn't look disturbed - and Vivian said that the behaviour I described wouldn't have been caused by rat poison. By now Vegas had started eating her hay.

Vivian said she thought the incident had been colic induced by the stress of getting stuck in the small barn section, and gave Vegas a jab to calm her stomach.

My beloved horse seems to be fine now. Just like Twiglet was in the end.

So there we are. What a morning. I feel very odd. And not very proud of myself. Beware of your Mama, my pets.

Laugh Conquers All
02/07/2014

So with three internet dating sites on the go, everything's going a bit mad. Possibly bad and dangerous to know as well. I'm having trouble keeping up, but I think I'm still on top of things, just. And anyway - after this sudden peak, I am fairly sure all will suddenly disappear and there will be nothing left, within days. But at the moment things are quite exciting!

The other night a chap of 41 who lived locally, and was so utterly drop dead gorgeous that he gave me butterflies, contacted me. I returned his message, and he turned out to be a Sikh from Leicestershire who had used a picture of a male model instead of himself, and completed an entirely fictitious profile, including describing himself as a 'white/Caucasian' living in Plymouth. Well what is the point of that? Just wasting everybody's time. All the same - I felt a bit spooked actually.

A day later an equally delicious young man of 34, Italian this time, contacted me, and looking at the pictures, I can tell from the background that he really is from Plymouth. But - now what? He's not brilliant at English and I can't imagine what we would talk about, or how he would make me laugh. I think he must be some kind of gigolo, but that is my suspicious mind.

Several of them write so utterly beautifully that you think they must speak like that too. And then they don't. Quite a lot of them look defeated and sad in their pictures, even though they all say, "I love life. I am just looking for a lady to share it with," in their profiles. And we're not 'ladies' - we're people. Calling us simply 'someone' would actually be fine. I hate the word 'lady'.

They nearly all seem to be terribly keen on honesty. I bet if honesty really hit them in the face (in the form of me, say) they'd run a mile. All the beaches that allow dogs must be packed out by lonely hearts enjoying what they 'love best', which is, apparently, 'walking their dogs'. 'I'm just a normal guy' doesn't do much to sell them to someone like me, 'who enjoys the good things in life like eating out, going to the cinema and theatre, as well as cosy nights in by the fire' drone on their cliché-packed profiles.

So far everybody I've come across on the internet seems to have some kind of major drawback.

Usually they are too old (I thought 60 should be my top limit - that's pretty old), too small, too fat, too bald, too glass half empty, or too boring. Annoyingly, I am also becoming increasingly convinced that it will only work for me with a privately educated person. Not that I'm particularly snobbish, but because ours is a little world of its own, where everybody has an automatic understanding of each other, including our own language. So that cuts out a mere 95% of the human race.

What does unite everybody that I have met is that they all, bar one or two, appear to be extremely nice, decent, well-intentioned people. Just like anyone that you might meet on the street really. Which they are, if you think about it!

And my guess is that if they really made me smile, giggle and laugh with uncontrollable mirth, any other concerns might well go straight out of the window.

So if it's inevitable that you must be flawed in some way if you're internet dating, what's my problem, you may well ask. Well it's obvious isn't it? There are no single men living anywhere near me. I am surrounded by nothing but sheep.

Beastly Boys
03/07/2014

Dear Faye was crying her eyes out and shaking with sobs, when I picked her up from school.

We seem to be having an emotional week, her and me.

A boy in the year above, with whom she has been at various schools since she was two, called her 'fat, with a low voice' in front of the little chap she love(s/d) most, and some of her other friends.

Nobody stuck up for her, and when she walked past, they all went quiet and stared at her.

Aged twelve she has learned something that I didn't learn until I was 50.

That few people put their necks on the line for you, whether they like you or not, in the presence of someone charismatic. I was more devastated by this discovery, than by almost anything else, when my marriage broke down. Faye will be much better prepared for the world.

Faye weighs the most in her year group. She is taller than the little squit who was being unkind to her. And his voice hasn't broken yet.

We went to look in the mirror together, and I explained the concept of body dysmorphia. "We are about the same fat, or not fat, aren't we?" I said to her, as we gazed at our joint reflections, "only you're without the tummy."

We're both statuesque, strong, robust people. Like Princess Diana might have been if she'd taken proper advantage of all those royal banquets.

My father was the President of the Boats at Cambridge. Faye and I would make good rowers, like her two stunning, willowy, 6' cousins who both rowed at Women's Henley last weekend. Faye agreed.

"Let's sing 'Feed the Birds'," I then suggested. She did so loudly, while I accompanied her on the piano, with as much exuberance as Liberace, but fewer sequins (and more mistakes).

"Sing that low G," I shouted at her over the din. She couldn't quite reach down to it. Her voice is not low enough. Just lower than the boy in question's.

The next day she was due to perform 'Let It Go', from the animated film 'Frozen', on her flute, in front of all yesterday's 'friends' at the School Summer Concert.

"You are truly going to Let It Go tonight," I informed her. "Are you allowed to wear mascara?"

"No," she replied.

"OK, put some on," I ordered. We tried on her old and new school skirt and jumper, and opted for the old one which is a little tighter, and she rolled up the kilt an inch or two. "And get yourself some new white socks from the school shop!" I shouted after her, as she got out of the car, ready to face down her unsupportive peer group.

Ex and Granny drove 4 ½ hrs and 2 hrs each way respectively, just to hear Faye's four minutes of fame.

The school dealt with the bullying incident first thing, reported back to me, and by evening, my dazzling dearly beloved daughter was up on that stage, with the widest smile lighting up her pretty face from ear to ear. She even closed her eyes dreamily, as she performed the very last crescendo of Let It Go, and we all went home for supper kindly cooked by Faye's ever-supportive loving Dad, before he left to go back to London, reaching his home at two in the morning.

Nice Philanderers?
03/07/2014

It must, by definition, be impossible to have an affair with a nice person.

Because if they were nice, before anything went too far, they would say, "Yes I feel the same as you do, but you must, must, must go back to your spouse - have counselling; do everything you can to keep the family together; do not betray your partner nor your children. As I must not betray mine. It would destroy us all. Go now, go, and we need never speak of this again."

Having an affair means that you must both behave dishonourably and dishonestly.

Viz (whatever that means, but Robinson Crusoe said it a lot) the secret relationship must be flawed from the beginning. And as a result, although obviously some affairs work out OK for everybody involved in the end, for the majority it would seem that the 'happy ever after' is terribly unlikely.

Personally, in my new romantic adventuring, I tend to go for 'dumpees' rather than 'dumpers'. Dumpees seem to have a more steady-neddy, sanguine approach to life; making the most of what is, and putting up with things, rather than nothing ever seeming quite good enough.

TripAdvisor's Gone Mad!
06/07/2014

Wydemeet's B&B reviews on TripAdvisor are so amazing that they make my tummy feel funny.

One after the other after the other. God - but they are so touching. Every time some new guests arrive I get butterflies and think to myself, "They are going to be disappointed; they are going to be disappointed. I can never live up to what it says on TripAdvisor."

So far, well. Phew! Everyone seems very happy. More than happy. Astonishingly happy! I am soooo chuffed! But still constantly nervous too.

Anyhow, I've just had this brainwave. All the internet dating sites seem so rubbish that perhaps TripAdvisor might present another public 'portal', if that's the correct 'now' word. So I just thought I would put in a little mention of my search for Mr Right on it. How cheeky is that?! I bet they censor it. Anyway - we'll see - I've just done it! FIngers crossed!

Bridget, Jeremy and Me
16/07/2014

The sort of people that I like, tend to have a general hatred of Bridget Jones, Jeremy Clarkson, Britain's Got Talent, and people who drive Range Rovers. As well as of the Daily Mail. So sadly, they probably won't go for me much either. Oh dear.

Here I am, lounging in the hot sun, next to the most enormous swimming pool, at Nielson's Holiday Resort, somewhere in the back of beyond in Turkey. I am immersed in the latest Bridget Jones book: 'Mad About The Boy', with Jeremy Clarkson's "Is It Really Too Much To Ask?" lying by my side, missing my Range Rover, and very much looking forward to tonight's 'Battle of the Bands" - this beach resort's version of BGT.

There are only two differences between me and Bridget Jones, I ponder.

One, is that she's a Mother Who Tries Too Hard, while I favour the Benign Neglect approach.

Two, is that she isn't real, whereas I am.

There are also two differences between me and Jeremy Clarkson.

I sometimes worry that I might upset someone.

I am not a bloke.

In this latest book, sadly Bridget Jones is not believable because she claims to be a Sloane but says 'toilet'. And also, a 29 year old hunky decent bloke falls for her via Twitter, without her even having posted a photograph. The chances of that ever happening are one in seventy-five trillion.

Bridget Jones' books are structured over a blog-type thought occurring every minute or two. Clarkson's all resound with, 'And there's the thing' every three pages, when he tells us how easily he could achieve world peace. Well I am hoping to copy both of them and turn this into a bestseller.

The problem is that if I succeed, the sort of people I like, won't like me.

Single Mum On Holiday
16/07/2014

"Might I join you?"

"No, we're having a family birthday party."

So I wander along to another table, with two couples sitting at it, and, again, nervously ask whether I might be able to take a seat there.

I swore never to attempt another sailing/beach resort holiday alone with my children, and here I am again, £4500 down, repeating the whole hideous experience.

At Nielson they have a special 'Social Table' in the dining area, which is the biggest one. I know that it's meant for all the singles, but in reality it's generally grabbed by the largest, happiest, most functional family groupings of all. Yuck. How inadequate do they make people like me feel? Honestly - I would be perfectly content all alone in a villa in the sun, miles from anyone, whereas this being surrounded by literally 100s of smug marrieds I'm finding very difficult.

Networking is my lifeblood, so I am used to pushing my way into anonymous gatherings, but a whole week of trying to find somewhere to sit, three times a day, at breakfast, lunch and dinner, invading what feels like other people's privacy and conversations, is becoming a total nightmare.

Occasionally one of my children, out of pity, might join me for breakfast, but that's it. If only all the people like me could be given badges to wear saying, "I'm desperate for someone to talk to," but I think I'm probably just the one person here who is!

The only single Dad I have met is Jake, who we bumped straight into on the transfer bus. He was once a professional weightlifter, and now he is a tooth implanter. He's got blond tinted hair, and is 51, but looks ten years younger.

He is here with his two sons, and is not interested in chatting to anybody; not even moi, because, he says, he spends all his working days making small talk to people who, with their mouths full of implements, can't reply.

There is increasing unrest in camp, shortly to become full rebellion I suspect, because it is advertised, amongst other things, as a sailing holiday, but no one has as yet been out in a boat. The quiet bay has turned into a surfing beach with onshore winds and huge waves, so the black flag's up and we're not allowed out.

Both children have turned feral and disappeared. So I have indeed met the main objective of this ghastly holiday, which was for them to thrive socially in their kids clubs. But it looks as though they're not going to learn to sail.

And at this rate, nor am I going to bump into a wealthy hearty six foot hunk of rich, single, posh Dad.

Eat Your Heart Out, Bridget Jones
16/07/2014

Units of revolting expensive Turkish wine: 502: fags: 111; Baklava calorie count: 15,432; minutes spent with children: 0; interesting conversations: 0; number of times giggled: 0; passes from Turkish waiters: 0; passes from English dads: 0; minutes spent sailing: 0; lengths swum: 20 (it's an Olympic sized pool); wardrobe malfunctions: 1: (my swimming costume is a small size 12); clouds: 0.

A Whole New Me
17/07/2014

In order to fit in to his kids club, Will (15) has changed his name and added a year to his age.

It's taken a couple of days, but he is already back to normal form, with his wraparound shades, baseball cap on back to front, and a trail of children wandering along behind him like the Pied Piper, children aged 16-18, some of whom are over 6' tall.

I woke him up for water-skiing this morning and commented, "Revered Son, you appear to have a large smear of mascara on your cheek." He grinned proudly. At lunchtime he was sitting next to a slim blonde goddess draped in diaphanous pink chiffon. His new friends reassure me that he is what I should refer to as a 'lothario', not a 'man-slag'.

Meanwhile my own new identity is, yet again, that of a pariah. I am now really struggling, particularly as I am used to being centre of attention. And one of the best looking middle-aged Mums of my various social groupings.

I mean, really. Normally I am so interesting that a screenplay has been written about me! But here everybody seems to see through me, as though I am made of air.

And they are all young and thin. Whereas I am old, wrinkly, fat, and generally unattractive in comparison.

I am finding myself walking around grinning to nobody in particular, and making pleasant small talk to every tom, dick and pillock, getting nowhere. Nearly all the other guests seem to be doctors and surgeons, so you'd have thought they'd be intelligent and interesting. But they're not.

Someone mentions the word NHS, if it is a word, at which point (Clarkson rant) they turn their backs on me in unison and have a competition as to who can squawk the loudest about how they're now working 210 times as hard as what they signed up for, their pay has been cut by 7,000% and their pensions have turned into 2 1/2p a year. As they buy another bottle of Turkish chardonnay for three million Turkish lire, and disappear off for an 'opi gel manipedicure', a 'Brush With Heaven' and back wax.

While I help myself to what's left of their wine.

What On Earth Is Happening To My B&B?
18/07/2014

TripAdvisor Ranking: 8 (going down); New Bookings: 0; Minutes spent worrying about this: 5.1/2; dates: 2

Oh dear. Here I am, basking in the Turkish sun, and I've just had a worry about what's going on at home.

A couple of days ago, just before Will, Faye and I set off on our mad trip here (I'd arranged a flight from Exeter to Manchester, followed by another to Dalman - forgetting that Will has a fear of flying - ending with a four hour coach transfer here, which is God knows where), a young couple arrived for their two night stay at my Dartmoor B&B.

We had tea and cake together, and they then set off, with no research, on the 1 1/2 hr each way hike across the moor to Princetown, wearing flip-flops, returning almost immediately in some distress as the female half of said couple had been bitten by a horsefly.

Faye provided her with antihistamine and then they went off somewhere in their car.

Meanwhile lovely Sally arrived. I found her through the Parish Magazine and I thought that she was so nice that all my guests would love her too. So I invited her to look after the house, dog, horses and guests, in no particular order, for the week while I was away.

As my children and I departed in Marvin, my Ford Focus, I had this terrible premonition that our new guests might have driven off in disgust, never to return! Thank goodness it was clearly me who had scared them away if so, rather than sweet Sally during her first hour of duties. What the Hell. I re-settle myself on my lounger, basking in the Turkish sunshine, still without a clue as to whether they returned or not!

So - back to today in Turkey:

1.32pm: Had lunch with widowed plastic surgeon from Harrogate (he specialises in burns rather than faces)

7.24pm: Still wondering whether my B&B couple ever came back.

7.25pm: Anticipating this evening's Event which is to be:

8.30pm: Turkish chef's Special Barbequed Goat Dinner, with widowed plastic surgeon from Harrogate, and Jake from Leicester.

Must wash hair and get out best spray-on black wraparound ancient t-shirt dress, and agonising matching patent sky high killer heels.

Just had a thought. Neither man is very tall.

Gee That's Better
18/07/2014

Number of people to stand me up: 1; Wine units: 227; Fags: 0; Barbequed goat calories: 3,456; Balaclava calories: 0; minutes spent in riveting conversation: 240; number of giggles: 10; number of passes by Turkish waiters: 0

Wow! What a night! Just what I had been hoping for!

Heads were turning knowingly over breakfast this morning, even though we had come down at different times. This is how it went:

8.50pm: I am wandering around the bbq dining area but can't tell who anybody is because I refuse to wear glasses or contacts. Plastic surgeon should be quite easy to spot because he is the only gentleman of mixed origin in the resort. Non. How disappointing. No one. I scour the bar area and finally alight on the silhouette of Jake the tooth implanter. He looks like a movie star.

9.00pm: We agree we have been stood up by plastic surgeon and enjoy our goat. Movie-star Jake comments with surprise: "You're funny". I don't suppose he has ever been forced to dine with a Size 14, six foot in her heels, 54-year-old FunnyMummy before. I giggle. A lot. How refreshing!

9.31pm: Acoustioke Night in the bar

10.23pm: Plastic Surgeon turns up. He says he waited for us, gave up and went to another beach bar for supper with the 'flotilla-mob'.

10.36pm: Ginger Bloke with Looks-Like-Me-Wife turns up. He's in the IT sector of the SAS or something, and tells us the story of how they managed to prove Shipman guilty, how Shipman continued to kill even from the confines of prison, and why it's not good nor funny that Will's best friend is able to hack into the school software system and change everybody's exam grades. Ginger Bloke is one of the most interesting people I have come across for a very long time.

1.00am: We all depart happily to our separate beds, except presumably, Ginger Bloke and his Looks-Like-Me-Wife.

Racing for Girls
20/07/2014

Lumps on head: 3: purple splodges on knees: 5; cuts on knees: 1; broken toes: 1 (maybe); muscles aching: all I have, plus more that I didn't know I had; missing tarty toe rings: 1; minutes spent with children: 0; passes from anybody, even girls: 0.

"Please would you give me a boat for girls," I pout coyly, my pretty sarong fluttering gaily in the gale, my bejewelled flip-flops sparkling on the wet sandy beach.

If I can't win through good sailing, I can win using girlie tactics. The eight most macho men of the resort, kitted out in black body armour, knuckle dusters and knee pads, and I, are choosing our Lasers (very fast and tippy sailing dinghies) for the Big Race.

At last the sailing is back on, and it's the most cut-throat event of the week - The Regatta.

Sure enough, I manage to take possession of the smallest girlie-Laser with the titchiest sail, which puts me in a class of my own, literally, tactics sorted; while the blokey blokes have to look macho so opt for bigger, faster, more gnarly (challenging) versions.

So I have already won the Laser 247 Class without setting foot in a boat, as

I'm the only one in it.

The red flag goes up indicating conditions are too dangerous for amateurs in single hulled dinghies.

Off 25 amateurs in single hulled dinghies charge, all attempting to start at the same time between two rather close-together buoys, and no brakes between us.

"Starboard!!" I scream, and the nicest, most dashing young Dad of the resort smashes into my boat, hard. "I thought you were meant to be good at sailing!" I hurl at him, struggling hard not to fall overboard. It's dinghy dodgems!

Two crashes and quite a lot of swimming later; I finally stagger in to shore - triumphant and exhausted. Sailing is so nice when it stops.

For the past hour I appear to have been using my head to physically move the boom backwards and forwards, smashing my knees on the bottom of the boat, and all the ropes or sheets or whatever they're called are tangled up, trailing out over the stern (back).

In the end, I came 8th out of all 25 competitors, once the handicaps had been applied, being the only Lady-in-a-Laser, and beaten only by Looks-Like-Me-Wife, (who was racing an easier boat), among the few female participants. Result!

Thank God that's sailing out of the way for at least another year.

Relax Hard
20/07/2014

I am the most beautiful person in Plymouth. Well not bad anyway.

But it would seem the ugliest in all of Turkey.

All these young marrieds I've been surrounded by for the last week have left me feeling old, unfit in both senses, very single, and generally past it (although still young and stunning when compared with the aquarobics class at my Plymouth Health Club).

And I think these beautiful people may be on the warpath. Quake in your boots, Nielson's! Your customers appear to be displeased that you have plonked the most glorious 5* £billion palatial hotel, meant for sailing, on what (on the face of it), seems to be a surfers' beach.

The company's strapline is 'Relax Hard' and that's just what most of their guests do. These people rise at dawn for water skiing (normally cancelled because of the windy, wavey conditions). Then it's mountain biking. Then tennis. Then weightlifting. Then fitness classes including my three perennial hates: Zumba, Aquarobics and Pilates. Followed by swimming, and sailing (generally cancelled). And then back to the first three. There is not an ounce of fat between them all. Except for Michael, one of the surgeons, who is so enormous that he has bosoms, and snores loudly on his sunbed.

At the end of the week there's a competition for 'The Most Perfect Family'. Jake and I pretend to vomit into our raki, but I am actually very jealous when my charming, bald friend (yet another surgeon, who I met when he was sitting down, and when he got up he turned out to be 5'4"), his lovely daughter and delightful wife deservedly take the honour.

I cannot imagine a more determined, intelligent, powerful force of people if this lot get the bit between their teeth. Even if most of them aren't very interesting.

They should be rounded up to sort out Putin and prevent World War 3, once they've dealt with Nielson's.

In the meantime, my diet starts the day the children begin their Autumn term.

I Hate Manchester
21/07/2014

"Are you expecting us to do some kind of ménage-a-trois or something?" I shouted, and I'm afraid to say I hurled the room key across the reception desk at the smug, dour, young scousers sitting behind it.

It was 3.30am Turkey time when we alighted on British soil. The first taxi at Manchester Airport had refused to take us to our hotel because 'they didn't know where it was'.

The second taxi kept driving for miles whilst I repeated 'Altrincham Road' over and over again, and dropped us at what turned out to be the wrong hotel in the opposite direction of where we were trying to go. It took ages for another taxi to come and £30 later we arrived at the Britannia Airport Inn, just down the road from the airport, as I had originally planned, complete with its indoor swimming pool.

Avoid! Avoid! Avoid!

The upshot of all that is it's now 3.30am UK time, and we are exhausted and fraught, rather than rested and calm, as I ask for the keys of the pre-booked triple room. There's already been two cock-ups with sorting out this hotel, because the agents originally booked me into the Gatwick Airport Inn rather than the Manchester one. Luckily I noticed on the booking form. I also noticed that they had only charged me £20 for the booking, instead of £117, which I kindly pointed out. They then, unkindly, didn't stick to their £20 quote (which I would have done, because I'm like that when I make mistakes).

Anyway - here we are now. The two young men surreptitiously glance at each other.

We open the bedroom door and they've given us one large bed with three sets of pillows on it. Will is an enormous hairy 15 yr old, and Faye scratches her eczema all night and kicks you in the head. This is a no-go, and very much not what I very specifically pre-ordered.

So, half an hour later, the young men sort us into three rooms, but mine hasn't been cleaned. Even I can't sleep in a stranger's sheets or use their towels.

So finally we are settled, as dawn begins to break.

My alarm clock is packed in Faye's suitcase on the other side of the hotel. And I can't order an alarm call because the phone doesn't work, and looks as though it hasn't for months.

In the morning the tv remote doesn't work.

At breakfast they have run out of mugs, bread (bread??!!) and bowls, my fruit salad is so old it's gone fizzy, yet breakfast time still has supposedly another hour to run. Meanwhile I hear the people on the next door table discussing how their hair-dryer has just caught fire.

Then, through the window, I see a rat running along the sill - oh no it's not, it's a MINK??!!

So I pop along for my recuperating swim and of course, there's no water in the pool.

You couldn't make it up. And I haven't.

What's Normal?
21/07/2014

We went to the Hurlingham Club-On-Sea, otherwise known as Polzeath Beach, today.

I was most relieved to discover that tummy and all, I didn't look particularly better or worse than all the other PLUs running about on the sand. Nielson Holidays must attract a sort of Aryan race. Or have curved mirrors. Phew.

Ping! Kerplunk!
30/07/2014

It was the hottest day of the year so far. We'd already been diverted a long way down tiny lanes, due to a crash.

We'd stopped at a garage to check the tyres, but nobody knew what pressure they were supposed to be.

And now I was panicking, my feminine glow dissolving into rivers of sweat, running down my face, my back, and under my arms. My heart started beating really fast and my tummy clenched.

Three tons of horse behind me, Will oblivious under his headphones in the passenger seat - and I couldn't steer.

Was I imagining things? We had to round another small corner and the car felt funny again. Help! I put on the hazard warning lights and slowed to a crawl up the 1:2 hill, as the engine started going twang, kerplunk, ping; and, after what felt like an eternity, and using all the strength in my arms, I just managed to manoeuvre us all into the new service station opposite Exeter Racecourse.

Calling the AA was top priority, but their card was lost after the last call-out to them just a couple of weeks ago, meanwhile my phone's battery was dying.

Eventually I got through, and they said they'd be out in two hours but could not take responsibility for the horses. It was 4.55pm on the Friday of a Bank Holiday Weekend, and all the car rental people would be going home in five minutes' time.

Unbelievably there was no phone number listed for the first Exeter 4x4 leasing place I managed to track down. But White Horse Motors, at 5.02pm, answered my call, and delivered the most enormous brand new Isuzu truck to me within 20 minutes. Meanwhile the AA arrived accompanied by a rescue van to take my old Nissan to a garage. They opened up the bonnet for a look.

"It's just a couple of snapped cables" they said. "That'll be £45 labour and the cost of the cables plus VAT to put right, ready by Tuesday."

At this point there were now two rescue trucks, the AA van, the Isuzu, the Nissan and the trailer all grouped together in the garage carpark. I was beginning to feel quite important! And a bit poor, as White Horse charged me £325 for their rental car.

Will, two horses, trailer and I were on our way again, on what should have been a relatively short journey to the livery near my Mum's. But now a giant juggernaut was taking up the entire tunnel in front of us.

One of us was going to have to reverse, and it wasn't going to be me.

That sorted, only to be met by an oversized tractor pulling a massive trailer of hay, in a tiny narrow lane. I was so exhausted I made the tractor driver get into my Isuzu and reverse it, complete with trailer.

We finally arrived at the horse livery just outside Beaminster, where I kept my first horse 22 years ago. A journey which should have taken two hours, had taken six.

But we had made it.

Wydemeet was satisfactorily rented out for the week, and my second holiday of the month about to begin!

Why Oh Why Oh Why Oh Why?
27/07/2014

Someone has been reading my blog! In fact two people have! Some hilarious comments have been left on it, which is proof! I've no idea who anybody is, but I'm chuffed to bits! And they're making me laugh!

But otherwise, today I find myself cross and frustrated. This is because it would appear that it is impossible to update my website and blog on my i-pad. Why?

Which means that I'm sitting here in my Mum's kitchen, bashing away on her Ancient Acer laptop, all because I've had to rent out my home to make ends meet as a result of an unwanted divorce, I've got nowhere else to go, and no access to my proper PC.

Yesterday I rang up my webhost people in America, at midnight, and yelled "Your country managed to put men on the moon 42 years ago (or was it? and did they actually, or was it all a conspiracy?) so why can't you make your stupid system work on the most popular and common tablet (or whatever it's called) of all in the whole world?" The bloke replied 'Have a nice day' and hung up.

I have written to Manchester City Council about their taxi operators, and they have written back predictably saying that without reference numbers they can't do anything. Rubbish. They can tell their drivers to learn English, learn their way around Manchester, and to smile.

I have written to Nielson who have predictably come back charmingly, saying they'll look into the matter of their sailing hotel being built on a surfers' beach, over the next 28 days.

I have written to the Manchester Airport Inn who predictably have not replied. I have also written them a review on TripAdvisor which is so rude that the TripAdvisor computer came back to me saying, "please press this button if you really meant to mention bedbugs in your review."

So I pressed the button.

I currently have court cases pending regarding Bill (my Shogun, more of that to come), BT, and a plumber from five years ago who is of no fixed abode.

My Angry of Wydemeet filing drawer is full to bursting, and I am finding being so permanently cross is very tiring and doesn't produce a flattering facial wrinkle formation.

What I don't understand is what other people do when they find themselves being treated as idiots, as happens to me so often. Do they just let it go, so that the perpetrators go on to rip off more innocent, gentle, busy people who aren't in a position to stand up to them?

Hymns and Pimms
31/07/2014

"The thing about Granny's house is that you think nothing bad can happen to you there," says Will.

I've done six days of holidaying at Granny's now, and I'm beginning to worry that I don't seem to have enough to worry about. I'm also struggling to manage on nine hours sleep, when I'm used to seven.

It's the sort of house where you can go upstairs in your wellies, and all the mirrors are speckly because Granny isn't really interested in appearances. Her face is a patchwork quilt of wrinkles, and her bony knuckles are of fascination to her young grandson. I dare say I shall look similar soon. At least I will be shorter than I am now - Granny has shrunk by about six inches so far.

But her home is calm and feels safe. Even all the in-laws, and ex-in-laws, find they can completely relax here.

Granny has been in a bit of a state for the past week because she is partially responsible for the annual Hymns and Pimms Evening tonight at the local church - where I got married 20 years ago, so I know that it seats precisely 70, as we personally measured each pew-size with our bums.

I read recently, or heard it on Jeremy Vine, that a chemical is released that makes you more anxious and cautious as you get older. Well that chemical has been released in Granny and I hope they have found an antidote for it by the time it's my turn.

Anyway - there must have been 70 people there, as the church was full. Granny read a lesson, and I felt a lump in my throat - as I would have if it had been 12 year old Faye, rather than 84 year old Granny. She had been up to the church earlier to practise, and it showed. My Dad, who used to train young Etonians to read in Eton College Chapel, would have been equally proud of her immaculate and dignified performance, watching us all, beaming, from his cloud in Heaven.

I was a bit unprepared that the hymns part of the evening turned out to include prayers as well - the less involved with praying I get, the odder it all seems. And I felt that I could have played the organ in a slightly more rousing fashion than the resident organist - although I have always found 'Jerusalem' a bit tricky.

And then, being Mum's daughter and on parade, despite having just got off a horse, I had to help, which has never been my strong point. I found myself handing round delicious smelling mini smoked salmon vol-au-vents, which, of course, I wasn't able to enjoy myself because both my hands were occupied holding the plate that bore them.

Well the thing is, it was really fun! And I just loved meeting Mum's local community. They are charming do-ers, mostly of my kind of age, and I am quite envious of her living amongst them all. One of them even personally knew two of the couples I've watched recently being featured on Channel 4's reality TV programme, 'Four In a Bed' - a competition for B&Bers that I'm tempted to take part in.

But the coup d'état was meeting a beautiful talented 16 yr old girl who sang a solo of the first verse of "I Vow to Thee My Country" even better than SueBo, who will be with Faye when she starts Big School next year, and who has already come across Will at some awful festival or other.

Post Hymns and Pimms, she was in touch with Will via Facebook even more quickly than I could manage to text him about her, and he will be cycling over to her house from Granny's, on his return from partying in SW6 tomorrow.

So church is still bringing people together, just as it did back in the days of Thomas Hardy.

Big Bertha
10/08/2014

"Snoop Dog was fantastic," reported 15 year old Will on his mobile this morning, "but the hurricane has blown down all the floodlights, and the campsite is such chaos it looks quite funny. The campervans are OK though."

He had saved up £180 from somewhere to join every other teenager in the south west, from the local butcher's apprentice, to good girls from safe schools, to posh cool kids from avant garde schools, like my son and his friends, to descend on the Boardmasters Festival at Watergate Bay, Newquay. And now the second day of festivities was to be abandoned, thanks to Hurricane Bertha.

The most interesting thing about this Festival, in my opinion, is what happens regarding sexndrugsnrocknroll. I had had considerable correspondence amongst the Mums of the four boys that I was delivering there - all of us trying to work towards a united approach on alcohol consumption.

Views varied from "We will impose a complete ban on any alcohol and trust them to keep to it," to "We will allow them a couple of bottles of lager and after that they will be left to their own devices as to how they are going to source anything else."

I was responsible for collecting the boys from the railway station, bringing them home to Wydemeet for the night, and then driving them on to the festival. I had reassured the Mums that the only supplies they could have access to would be provided by the sheep outside my gate, or stolen from my Cellar of Plonk.

The Festival organisers, we understood, had imposed a complete ban on spirits, and a maximum of 12 cans of lager per adult, and no alcohol for

Under 18s. Meanwhile the social media were alive with ruses for smuggling in booze; and that ghastly NOS stuff (laughing gas) - that Mums take during childbirth, and it jolly well didn't make me laugh.

Have you seen those pictures of pretty teenage girls in their LBD's breathing in and out of coloured balloons to enjoy a brief, legal, and apparently relatively safe and inexpensive high? They look absurd. The suppliers describe and sell the equipment as being useful for whipping cream. Eh? I think we used to make soda water with it in the '70s.

Anyway, apparently the way to smuggle NOS into these festivals is to stuff the canisters, which you've bought for £7.50 off eBay, up the hollow metal legs of your picnic chair. Bottles of booze are incorporated into a carved out loaf of sliced bread, or the drink is decanted into a punctured coke can re-sealed with a glue gun. My feeling is that these adolescents are more excited about how to outwit the security men than in the taste of alcohol, or in breathing nitrous oxide.

On the way to the Festival I had to buy some croissants from Morrison's, some sausages from the butchers, and collect the laundry for my B&B.

"You can all buy your lunch while I collect the croissants," I trilled merrily to my young passengers.

I reached the till with my purchases. Ooooops. What had I just done? I'd proactively delivered the fearsome four into what to all intents and purposes was an offy!

"You see those four boys over there?" I hissed to the till assistant. "Well they're all 15."

Hah - got them!

She pressed a flashing light and pointed to her badge which stated that anyone appearing under 25 would be asked for ID. "I would have stopped them anyway," she reassured me. So all they came out with were some sandwiches and a packet of crisps. (I think.)

Tax Credits Are Stupid
14/08/2014

"£5,472.27 is due from you now."

That's what an innocent-looking letter from HM Revenue and Customs says, that I've just this moment opened.

What???? Who has that sort of money just hanging around?

I'm so cross I think I'll buy a car.

It's taken a year or so for the Tax Credits people to catch up with themselves and decide that I don't deserve to have been given the money after all.

Obviously it's completely nuts that they ever paid me credits in the first place. That was because they don't count spousal maintenance - however much you get. Even if it's millions a week!

But the reason they're asking for £5,000+ back is equally nuts. I'm lucky enough to have come into an inheritance, but it's currently being used to pay off its own death duties, so I won't actually receive anything at all from it for practically a decade. Yet that does count.

Twats. No wonder the country's in terminal decline.

Golden Monster
14/08/2014

I know everything about tow vehicles.

For a start, I now know that that is what they are called. I learned all about them on Tuesday, and bought one this morning.

Some of the perceived pros and cons of different makes and models are, of course, personal; and some depend on where you live and the job you want doing.

First and foremost, after my recent experiences with the ancient Nissan Terrano, I was after something reliable, in which I could feel safe pulling my two horses in their trailer up the hill past The Forest Inn, at the end of my lane. This has a One in Two gradient, is one car wide, and has a blind corner.

And I wanted a diesel automatic. It must cost less than £6000 and should have fewer than 100,000 miles on the clock.

As a result of these criteria, my search on eBay, AutoTrader, Exchange & Mart, Pre-Loved, Gumtree, and something called 'Motors', narrowed right down to just a few cars in the whole of the UK.

I believe Land Rover Defenders, Discoveries and Range Rovers tow better than anything - they're rated up to 3.5 tons, 'braked'. But I don't want any of them, because according to the online chat forums they're always breaking down.

I LOVE Toyota Land Cruisers.

Shoguns are man enough.

And then there's something called a Kia Sorrento, which the horsey ladies on the Horse & Hound website swear by.

By now I was down to about 25 vehicles in the entire country.

So off I set yesterday to try out a Sorrento in St Austell, an Isuzu Rodeo (more comfortable, better turning circle, more reliable than the Nissan Navarro and Toyota Hilux, I read) in Plymouth, a Land Cruiser in Exeter, and another Sorrento in Tiverton.

The first Sorrento felt like a big powerful box on wheels. "If you want a truly awful car that is a cheap means of towing 3.5 tons, this is the one for you," read the blurb. I quite liked it, but it got stuck in low gear 4 wheel drive. Not a promising start.

The Isuzu (how do you pronounce that?) D-Max was golden. GOLDEN??!! Imagine me turning up in this F-off truck as big as a football field, at the Pony Club! I mean it's bling gone mad! Nevertheless, I got in it and it felt like a new car. 2006 reg with 69,000 miles on the clock, VAT included, used by one lady owner (the salesman's auntie) to tow her horses occasionally. A bit different from a truck used daily in the mud by a farm labourer wearing his hobnailed boots. Its size and power would mean that it wouldn't even feel a heavy trailer attached to the back, and stinky tack could go in the separate covered boot.

I was also very taken by the bloke selling it. He was a proper professional salesman - young and nice-looking in his beach shorts and flip-flops, chatting away, like we were old friends, about his family (his brother won the Grand National on Seagram) sounding oddly like a cross between Ricky Gervais and that tall west country cohort of his in 'Extra's'.

I am a complete sucker for professional sales techniques, and was particularly impressed by the clearly genuine pride he takes in his vehicles, pointing out everything that he felt wasn't 100%, such as a couple of scratches, a bald tyre, a lock, and valeting, all of which were to be sorted out the following day.

Then I went to see the Land Cruiser in Exeter. 1999 reg. It had rusty windscreen wipers, two tyres in need of pumping up, and looked old, sad and forlorn, even though it only had 99,000 miles on the clock. The seller didn't bother to return my five phone calls and wasn't there when I arrived.

The owners of the second Sorrento still haven't returned any of my phone calls, but in the description it says that the low 4x4 gear light stays on. Hmmmm. Sounds as though there might be a problem with that car.

I reminded myself that the garage selling on my beautiful Range Rover insisted I paid for £3000 worth of work before they were prepared to display it on their forecourt. So I thought, "No, I am buying something in perfect working order from a garage which has given the car a full service and provides a three month guarantee." And went home.

Well you may remember my worry that I like people who don't like Range Rover drivers?

Yet now I've gone and bought the Golden Monster. The supreme, ultimate, definition of bling. What on earth are they going to think about that?

I've Fallen in Love!
18/08/2014

I could hear the throbbing through the bathroom window, and looking out, there was his helicopter approaching. My latest internet date was dropping by for a coffee - circling the property, checking out the white tea-towel Sashka had put in the top of the horses' field to act as a landing strip, while I lay in the bath.

We have had several visitations from friends in helicopters over the years. Every time, they never fail to cause the adrenalin to pump. Those little machines are just so loud, and their propellers go round so very fast; I find the whole thing hugely exciting!

The reason why I was still in the bath was that my date's and my definitions of what constitutes 'mid-morning' clearly seemed a bit awry.

Which meant that strapping, tall, blonde Sashka had to go out to the top of the field to greet him. I bet he thought she was me!

He had described himself as being 68, but in fact, when I checked him out on Google afterwards, he's actually 73.

After we'd all waved goodbye I drove off in Ken, the ancient Nissan Terrano, part-exchange, to collect the Golden Monster.

Well. I tell you. I've fallen in love. I just LOVE this new car. It's unmissable. Unusual. Rather in your face. But steady, safe, reliable, practical, and does the job. Just the same as me.

I have never had a car so new.

It's got a little gadget called 'Parrot' in it, which I dare say will turn out to be very useful when my children show me what it does; and I have worked out how to plug my phone in so I can listen to my own music. Loudly.

And I can take this wonderful truck back to the garage for servicing at cost, while they provide me with a courtesy car.

It's so comfortable, and such a pleasure to drive, that now I'm doing the sums to work out whether it makes sense to give away Marvin the Magic Focus, and use the Golden Monster as my runabout instead. But all the tables on Google are in litres/kilometre so I really can't work out the sums!

Dead
05/09/2014

"Just look at this brilliant thing!" I gushed.

The key in the lock went "click click click" and then nothing.

This was to have been my third outing in the Golden Monster. The children and I were on our way to Cornwall for the evening, to meet Judith and her new Encounters boyfriend, for a swim at their hotel on the very beautiful, relatively ignored, Rame Peninsula, just across the river from Plymouth.

The next day was Pony Club Camp Day - Bank Holiday Monday. A two hour drive away, pulling both horses in their trailer - for which I bought the Golden Monster in the first place.

We all quickly decamped into Marvin the Focus and off we set.

Next morning my two lovely guests, together with Geoffrey, who does all my mending, stood around the Golden Monster in the pouring rain, attempting to jump-start him from their Discovery, but to no avail. So it was that the AA visited me for the tenth time in two years.

I think I have probably reached the limit of my allowance of visits. The nice man started my new truck OK from his powerful batteries, and then we had to leave it running, with a brick holding down the accelerator, while I finished serving breakfast, found someone prepared to replace a 3 litre diesel battery on a Bank Holiday; as well as a farrier, because Mad Vegas had chosen this day of all days to lose a shoe.

Halfords! I love them! £126 and three hours later we were packing up the car; a farrier had been found who had driven all the way from Torquay - and I set off with the two horses and Faye to join fifty other children for a week's camp in the Somerset rain.

I'm sure this was just a one-off blip on the part of Golden Monster.

House of Love
05/09/2014

I had to meet Malcolm's new partner last week.

He found her through Guardian Soulmates. She lives in Totnes. She'll be a crystal-gazer, then. She'll have straggly, unwashed, unbrushed, long, thin, maroon hair with grey roots, wear floppy brown clothes all made from natural fibres, and on her feet will be hideously expensive, individually handmade, leather, Cornish pasty shoes. She'll exude the smell of musk, joss-sticks and what my son refers to as 'weed'. And she'll be a Vegan Liberal Socialist.

Sigh. Better quickly mow the lawn between storms. And be late on purpose. And deliberately rude.

I roar up outside the quiet country pub in my huge new bling truck, and replace my bright pink wellies with some sober and tasteful sparkly blue flip-flops.

I walk in, there they are, and ping! She has something about her. I really like her. Immediately. Before she has even said anything. One of those unusual special people who exude an aura of calm, smiling, gently humorous, modest self-assurance. She's also got more hair than me, and is thinner, and trendier too, even though she is two years older. She's wearing those undone little gym shoes with no laces.

She is so funny. She really makes me laugh. She and Malcolm feel like grown-ups indulging a kid, and I am allowed to be loud and to show off, and to be enjoyed. She is great. She is going to come riding with me soon. I am so glad that he is in such a safe pair of hands.

Ex also has a new girlfriend, predictably ten years younger than him, and according to everyone I've pumped for info, looking a bit like me only smaller. Faye gets on well with her daughter, and both my children like her. I had thought Ex would choose well when he eventually found someone whom he was happy to introduce us to. I have invited Ex to ask her to stay, but I don't suppose he'll be doing that in a hurry.

I have deliberately chosen to surround myself with romantic couples who either completely get what staying with me is all about, and love Wydemeet for its remoteness, beauty, comfort, peace, and amazing surrounding wilderness. Or they're wondering where the wardrobes are and why there are bats in the trees.

Which leaves me. On my own. My love-life becomes ever more rubbish. I forgot to cancel Encounters, so I am still a subscriber to that, but my Guardian Soulmates subscription has recently run out. Just as well - the past three 'likes' I received came from ugly men of varying strange religious persuasions. I emailed them back saying "I read the Daily Mail so I don't think you would like me."

Last night I sent a message to a hunk from Oxford who claimed to like all the arts, both highbrow and lowbrow.

I said, "What - even X-Factor?"

He replied with: "I haven't been lobotomised!"

I thought that was rather good so I came back with: "Pity, I love X-Factor. Clever you to be able to spell lobotomised."

Anyhow - this morning I discover that he has 'blocked' me!! I have never been blocked before. So I can't get back to him to explain that I am extremely civilised and erudite, despite my penchant for all things Cheryl Cole (or Fernandez or whatever she calls herself now). As well as Simon Cowell. He is a living legend.

My take on it is this. If you imagine you are at Exeter College with 2000 people of the same age and in the same kind of world as yours, and it's still tricky to find a suitable boyfriend or girlfriend, then it's no wonder that online dating can prove a bit slow, when there's only a handful of like-minded, single, available people of the same generation, living within a 200 mile radius of yourself.

Your other choice, of course, is sheep. But they're nearly all ewes.

Wasting Time
05/09/2014

I have written five blogs today.

I've also had three mugs of coffee, and finished up two small slices of old chocolate cake, meant for my B&Bers, designed to look home-made by the lady in Tavistock market, but actually she cooks her cakes in bulk, using margarine instead of butter.

But I've had no fags.

And I'm not on a diet either. Big decision. I have agreed with myself - what's the point really? I would rather go out with someone fat, than starve myself for someone who at present doesn't even exist. Some people like me the way I am, anyway.

And all of this is despite my post-summer holidays 'to do' list being three pages long.

Because I am putting off 'It'.

'It' being the court's forms for my two litigious cases - one against the Okehampton garage who claim to have mended Bill the Shogun when they haven't - after all these months there's still a flashing little yellow light on Bill's dashboard where there shouldn't be, so I've had to buy the Golden Monster; and the other is against BT. Both cases are scheduled to come up in court in November.

The whole process involves Small Print. Being Meticulous. Psyching yourself into a righteous rage. Urrgghh.

Tired and Happy
07/09/2014

Some time ago Ex and I reached a kind of truce.

It was based on the principle that if everything we do is in the best interests of the children, then there is no room left for argument. So we don't. Argue that is. Provided the subjects of Her, and Money, are avoided at all times.

I would like to imagine that this arrangement might work for many estranged parents, although I know it doesn't for those of my friends who made the unfortunate mistake of marrying complete nutters.

So as you've probably realised already, Wydemeet B&B exists primarily to fund the children's school fees.

These have already been covered once, but got swallowed up in the divorce, so I've had to save up for my half all over again. Bummer. Except that I've found that I like doing the B&B. And just as important, the children enjoy their schools. And they like the B&B too.

Never mind that Will occasionally can't have a shower because it's been cleaned ready for guests. And sometimes he has to share his bedroom with his Dad, and not play his music too loud. And/or sleep in the shed if I need his room.

He has discovered, somewhat to his surprise, that the people who come to stay tend to be rather nice, and he quite enjoys carrying up bags and making cups of tea and chatting to them. Most of the time though, our guests are asleep when he's awake, and awake when he's asleep.

Ex 'gets it' and does his bit too, without complaint. A set of guests once commented, "Gee I hear a polar explorer once lived here!"

I replied "Yes, he's serving your breakfast tomorrow!"

Today has been a bit of a red letter day on the children front, more particularly for Faye.

First, we had the hunter trial at the Pony Club.

Faye completed a confident fast clear round on my horse, Perfect Panda, and didn't cry once!

Meanwhile our 'problem horse' Vegas WON!!! Out of a field of 31! Hah hah. That will show everybody who's so horrid about her. She should be called Marmite.

Later in the afternoon, bolstered by an hour's Disney Channel, Faye played Leonard Cohen's 'Hallelujah' on her flute, and hallelujah indeed! We now have Faye's potential music scholarship piece in the bag.

We're both going to bed very tired and very happy.

I Can Breathe Again!

11/09/2014

Yesterday I drove past Her house (I have to drive past it almost daily for the school run, shopping in Tavistock etc), hoping to see a 'For Sale' sign.

How incredible that in five years, what She has done has never been discussed between us, or even acknowledged, let alone apologised for, despite our being thrown together several times a week. And now it never will be, as the rumour is that She's off to London. Hurray!!

The new school merger has resulted in Faye finding herself being taught Latin by her favourite teacher in a class comprising solely her four best mates.

There have been other, less constructive changes at the school, such as the children being made to learn a song called "I love broccoli" in preparation for Harvest Festival. Give me 'Fight the Good Fight' any day. But by and large, I have never seen the school's remaining original teachers wearing wider grins, or cracking worse jokes!

Last Friday, at a new school bonding drinks party, I ensured that I made the acquaintance of the new headmaster's wife, and then the
new headmaster himself, who found himself stuck with me for 40 minutes.

Where were all the other pushy parents I panicked, making more and more of a fool of myself, staring at his rugby player chest, remembering crying onto his predecessor's one on several occasions.

Eventually I made my excuses, seeking out the new head of the junior school, only for him to run away from me as he did last time I tried that.

Not sure what it is about me. But I think I have just scuppered any chances Faye might have had of becoming Head Girl of her newly formed school.

Life Enhancer
15/09/2014

My goddaughter has just taken the best picture of me that I have ever seen! So what choice did I have but to re-subscribe to Encounters? After all, it's only £32 for a month, and could change my life for ever.

I thought you might be a bit curious as to how I've described myself on my 'Profile Page', so here it is:

WHY SHOULD PEOPLE GET TO KNOW YOU?

I'm good-looking, confident, clever, charismatic, sorted, solvent, sexy, posh, educated, easy-going, funny, cheerful, warm, empathetic, decent and loyal, modest and humble.

WHAT ARE YOU LOOKING FOR?

You see the bigger picture. Clichés are not really your thing.

You are highly articulate, know what you want and like, and are so comfortable in your own skin that you don't care very much what other people think.

You are very strong and confident, with a terrific sense of humour and a ready, warm smile.

If you are a trifle egocentric, I don't care - you are entitled to be. I will respect you and support you, and together we can achieve the impossible if we feel like it - hand in hand. Or just eat scallops pronounced scollops somewhere nice - I hesitate to say 'in front of the fire'.

People will love us as a couple because we are friendly, funny, exciting and dynamic. I will enjoy that, but you won't be particularly bothered one way or the other. etc

I am now hoping to be inundated with messages.

Name-ist
23/09/2014

I think a person's name usually tells you a lot about them.

Most of the people on Encounters have perfectly normal names, as you might expect.

They send me charming, erudite messages, and couldn't be nicer, better looking, or more intelligent.

In fact of the many blind dates I have met, there's only one that I haven't liked. And no crazy people at all - yet, anyway, as far as I can tell.

I've been dying to fall for all of them, but annoyingly, I know straight away that it's not going to work if their name's not right.

For instance, I have a problem with anyone whose name starts with 'K', and with abbreviated names.

People called Kevin or Dave will be bored stiff by my world of private schools and horses. They will never understand why I spend all my money on school fees, thus ensuring that my children will never fit into the real world. How could they, when I don't?

Last week I talked schools with three other Mums for five hours. On visiting the used-coffee room and surreptitiously checking my watch, it said 1.40pm, so I asked Diana what the real time was, and she said that was it.

It was my 55th birthday and we had been enjoying coffee, and a birthday cake with those candles that you can't blow out. In the end we had to dunk the candles in the teapot before they set light to the hotel.

So now I'm name-ist, height-ist, thin-ist (I don't want someone to fall over if I hug them), fat-ist, and age-ist.

All of which cuts down my chances of finding true love to almost zero.

The other thing that isn't great for my success rate is that several potential suitors object to being lied to.

Although normally instinctively honest, when it comes to internet dating profiles I think there is a different moral code. I've said I'm 49, so that I appear in the 'Women aged 40 - 50' category.

I've also put down that I never smoke. Well - it's only the occasional one.

Finally I ticked boxes for: I have no sense of humour, I wear bifocals, my favourite colour is brown, my favourite clothes are my Granny's cast-offs, and I've got a beard.

It's a Hard Life
28/09/2014

I bought a return ticket to Gerona for £80, for three days of doing nothing under a murky sun at my Norwegian best friend Lindsey's house, hidden away on a totally unspoilt part of the Mediterranean coast in Northern Spain.

Staying with her turned out to be cheaper than being at home! And then I found out how much it had cost to leave the Golden Monster at Bournemouth Airport. £105!!

But who cares really. I was just so, so tired after a B&B August.

"Please, Mary, if I drive the car up to the gate, won't you even come and visit the nudist beach just down the road? It's really beautiful and no walking involved, and you don't have to take your kit off..." Lindsey had pleaded with me. But I just couldn't move. She thought I'd gone a bit mad. But actually I was just totally, utterly exhausted.

On my arrival, Lindsey had announced that a Hollywood Superstar would be joining us for dinner.

"I will have a shy-on," I fussed.

Well. Who would have guessed. It turned out that the icon of glamour, now living down the road from Lindsey, used to be my neighbour in the middle of nowhere in Devon! At the height of her fame in one of those American soap operas, she would escape to 'Little Sherberton' - a shack without plumbing, reached by driving across a field at the end of my lane! Nobody ever knew she was there!

After posting my new pic and re-subscribing to Encounters, all went mad, and those three blissful days in Spain were spent replying to 1000s of messages, gazing at the view across the harbour and out to sea.

Back at Wydemeet, two hours turnaround time and we're off to a 7pm dressage lesson for Faye, horse in tow, an hour away. Returning to bed at midnight. Again.

What It's All About
29/09/2014

I had one of those moments the other day.

When you remember what it's all about, and why you bother.

I had been out for an organised evening ride on the western part of the moor near Tavistock, everyone was heading for home, and the time had come for my mare, Panda, and me to turn around and return, alone, to our trailer.

Perfect Panda, who hadn't been out with other horses for months, was fed up that she had been made to go so slowly for such a long ride.

As we turned, she leaped into a fast gallop, flying across heather, gorse, ditches, bogs and rocks, the sun sinking slowly behind us, so that the colours of the moor gradually mutated from greyish into dark greens, yellows, oranges and deep reds. I remembered how not to fall off, as we careered as one, back to the battered old trailer, at 30mph. Eventually we arrived back at the oasis which is our beautiful home, uniquely located right in the middle of the moor, to find it bathed in moonlight.

Sometimes, being alone is Good.

3 GETTING NOWHERE, SLOWLY

Sex Wax
29/09/2014

The entire house had begun to reek of coconut. It was becoming truly disgusting!

So I called up Will and said, "The entire house is beginning to reek of coconut. Why?" Will likes the smell of coconut - he thinks it smells of cool surfing, and I believe a lot of his Lynx products are flavoured with it. When I was his age the equivalent was Brut. I used to sniff my 17 yr old boyfriend's spotty neckerchief which was drenched in the stuff. I still love that smell now!

Meanwhile, I think coconut smells of 15 year old son, and I don't want it wafting around the parts of our home that guests occupy.

Will said, "There's a small piece of cardboard hanging from the lamp in my bedroom at the top of the house. It's called 'Sex Wax' and you can move it to the Bothy outside, if you like."

Well I did just that, and the awful aroma disappeared straight away.

I daren't open the door of the Bothy again though, as I might faint! At least it will no longer stink of tobacco and joss sticks. But I am now worried that this 'Sex Wax' thing's smell is going to start permeating around the garden and everyone will think they're on a beach!

Eating Ponies
07/10/2014

There's been a lot of discussion in the media recently about tucking into sandwiches made from cuddly-wuddly Dartmoor foalies.

I think it was my mate, Charlotte Faulkner, who first went public on the subject. Charlotte founded The Dartmoor Hill Pony Association nearly twenty years ago, and no one could care more passionately about the moorland ponies than she does. With endless loyal support from her extended family, she has devoted the latter part of her life to their cause.

I know quite a lot about marketing meat because I used to work for the British Turkey Federation, so I'm particularly interested in all of this.

In our promotional materials we would never use pictures of squidgy-widgey live turkeys. Our job was to divorce completely the idea of the cling-filmed slab of cream fillet in the supermarket from anything that had ever been alive. I eventually stopped sending press releases to The Independent (the least independent newspaper of them all). At least nobody reads it except journalists) because they would simply use my info as a catalyst to call up their friends at 'Chickens Lib' (yes it does exist), and give poor old Bernie Matthews another roasting.

I have even turned down opportunities to appear on the Today programme, because I know they're just after a slanging match between the turkey people and the veggies, which is never going to sell more turkey sausages.

So I was a bit horrified to see on our local BBC Spotlight programme a large slithery piece of red pony fillet being swirled around in a bowl of what looked like dark red blood, but I think was actually wine, interspersed with shots of merry foals gambling on the moor and licking tourists' ice creams.

However, on the Jeremy Vine Programme it was a relief to hear about 95% listeners talking sense.

The only two against grilled Dartmoor pony cutlets were both clearly barmy wimmin. They sounded quite mad before they'd even reached their bit about pony-eating.

Charlotte is clear about the real problem of not having enough ponies on Dartmoor, which has been somewhat overlooked in most of the media's coverage of the subject. Ponies keep the moor in good order. They eat scrub - gorse, bracken etc - that even the sheep won't touch. With numbers of ponies down from 30,000 to 3,000 or something, the speckled warbler is apparently thriving - good for it, but being understocked, the moor itself is becoming ever less accessible for walkers, riders, cyclists, farmers etc, the heather is disappearing, and at the bottom line - it's less beautiful than it was when we first moved to Wydemeet in 1995.

The Dartmoor commoners continue to maintain some ponies. But the majority of the foals get shot, and fed to the hunt hounds, or their carcasses are torn to bits by zoo animals. Why shouldn't they be nicely packaged up for human consumption?

Unlike the millions of hot housed chickens and turkeys we consume, the lucky, pretty Dartmoor foals have a jolly, free life til it comes to their crunch.

Oxygen
08/10/2014

Today is Goosey Fair - an historical event put on annually by the attractive Devonian market town of Tavistock.

The first time I went I was rather hoping for a goose sandwich - I rather like goose. Makes a change from Dartmoor Pony, or turkey for that matter.

Well, there was not a goose in sight, I searched and searched. Instead I came away with five watches (all of whose batteries expired five months later), and a pair of slippers in Size 8.

The staff and Mums at Faye's school dread Goosey Fair, which is held on the first Wednesday of October every year. I'm the only one I know who looks forward to its buzz and naffness.

Of greatest interest to me is the almost universal inverse relationship between precocious child and scary ride. Faye's best friend Jocelyn is a slight, gentle, very polite, obedient and intellectual creature, meanwhile determination and courage do not feature at the top of the leader board for Faye, when it comes to the hockey pitch or the cross country course.

And yet. These two, aged 10, insisted on queueing up for the scariest rides available at the fair. The tallest, fastest, highest, loudest one is called 'Oxygen'. Diana (Jocelyn's mother) and I both felt sick as we stared up at our two little girls whizzing around backwards and forwards and upside down, 200 metres above us, laughing their heads off.

Their Alpha peers waited next to us at the foot of the horrifying, thumping, crane-like edifice, gazing up in wonder, a newfound respect emerging for our sweet daughters. Then they quietly slid off to their own favourite ride - one where you sit in a giant teacup and, very slowly, go round in circles.

Another Country
21/10/2014

Miles driven: 650; time spent driving: a couple of weeks; coffees consumed: 25; fags consumed: 25; taxis paid for because late for school pick-up for Beloved Daughter: 1; new boyfriends attained: 0; MPG: 40!!!

"We are from the same world, but inhabit very different countries."

Like a total moron, having corresponded with him for hour after hour, week after week, writing all sorts of hilarious stuff especially for him, I drive six hours each way to Cambridge to see him, and two days later I get dumped by text without even a "but you are pretty", or "thank you for coming all this way"!! I ask you! AND I had stopped off en-route for a quick spot of TK Maxx therapy, in Slough where I was born so don't be rude about it, but why on earth my mother couldn't have chosen Royal Windsor like she did for my siblings I will never know, and I have to admit to my Place of Birth on at least one form a month ... anyway, where was I?

So first I was hurt. Then I was a bit affronted. But all the time I knew he had a point, which I think he expressed in a rather perceptive and concise way, as opposed to going round the houses. I have actually started using the expression myself, as a quick, easily understandable and not too rude way to fob off the 98% of inappropriate people who contact me online.

During our meeting, I had quietly admired his nicely ironed striped shirt, his shiny cufflinks, orange socks and light tan brogues. I thought they matched my Golden Monster rather well. And he was considerably taller and heavier than I am. I just love that.

So. Sigh. The thing is I belong everywhere and nowhere. I don't actually have a 'country'. Anyone who isn't posh thinks I am. And anyone who's genuinely posh knows I'm not. And there's no-man's land in-between.

So I think this annoying bloke has hit it on the head in a sentence.

My 'country' currently comprises a great deal of chat about private schools, swimming, riding, doing lunches, school run, watching children's matches and events... And running a successful B&B business.

How do I provide time to make a man feel special in and amongst all of that?

Nine out of Ten Judges Prefer Me
06/11/2014

Dah-doing, dah-doing, dah-doing. That was my heart going at 180 beats a minute.

I paid another little trip to the Ladies.

I have often been told that it doesn't show when I'm nervous.

I hoped it wasn't showing now.

I was outside Court Room No 2, sitting a stone's throw away from my adversaries, waiting to be called in by the judge.

"Odd," I thought. "I feel just like this when I'm stuck in the same room as my Nemesis, only I don't hate them as much as I hate Her. I just don't want to look at them and will pretend they don't exist."

My next thought was, "This waiting outside The Room of Judgement must be what being on The Apprentice feels like."

The internal phone rang.

"Hadow vs Thingy. Lord Whateverhisnamewas will see you now."

We followed the receptionist lady into a large, high-ceilinged chamber, with My Lord sitting way above us behind a barrier on a sort of platform at one end, surrounded by microphones.

"You may sit down," the elderly gentleman from my sort of world commanded from his stage.

"Yes M'Lud" gushed the garage-man, a short, fat, t-shirted version of Uriah Heep.

Well the outcome was always obvious. Two hours later the judgement was that the garage should keep Bill, my knackered Mitsubishi Shogun, and return the £2500 I had paid them despite their not repairing him properly, plus £275 I had paid in court costs.

All just as anyone sensible could have predicted months ago. The whole thing was a complete waste of everybody's time, money, and nervous energy. A pyrrhic victory. I did not in the least feel like jumping around grinning and punching the air, as they wrote me out my cheque. Instead I felt like hitting them. Stupid, thick, idiots.

What was most interesting to me about the whole experience, was how the garage man's bottle blonde girlfriend streamed lies - so many that I couldn't keep up and remember them all when it was finally my turn to be allowed to speak. Under no circumstances may you interrupt either the other party, nor the judge. And if you start writing things down you can't keep up.

Amongst 1000 other things, she claimed that, when I had driven all the way to the garage to discuss the situation, my "man friend" and I had both been aggressive towards her, that I had thrown the car keys at her, and run out of her office.

In fact I had thought that my "man friend" Peter – with the sports car - who had very sweetly agreed to accompany me into the fray, and was keeping out of the way near the door, wasn't actually as supportive as I had expected he might be.

Meanwhile, far from 'throwing the keys down', I had actually left them in the car for the garage to check out what was still wrong with it, and subsequently driven off with kind Peter in his MX5 for a delicious lunch at the Mill End Hotel outside Chagford.

I think, though, that she believed every word she was saying, despite even the judge appearing to raise his eyebrows slightly. He termed my communications with the garage staff as "unsatisfactory" and it was fairly clear to me that he had a pretty good idea of what had really happened.

I wonder whether hours and hours and hours and hours and hours of court time are wasted like this every day.

I put the problem down to education. The pair were just, simply, massively THICK, and I can't hate them for that. I know that I am privileged to have received a first rate education and am automatically at an advantage.

I have now won nine of the ten of my small and middle-sized claims over the past decade or two. These include the cutlery company whose 'lifetime' silver plate went green after less than a year; two plumbers; BT (twice); a holiday company who neglected to supply the aeroplane home, a removals company who left behind half our belongings, and whose lorry we had to push up the hill in the snow; and an ex-friend for whom I bought a horse, who sold it without telling me and sniffed the proceeds up his nose. Most of them were already bankrupt and knew just how to avoid the bailiffs, so I haven't necessarily received compensation, but I do feel that they have had some sort of come-uppance.

The one case that I have lost was with the burglar alarm company who charged double their estimate without checking first that I would be prepared to pay that much, so I didn't. They sued me, and I now have a credit rating problem because I was on holiday when the order arrived telling me to cough up.

So my question is, why am I the only person I have ever met who gets herself into these situations? I may be a blonde (a real one), but I won't put up with people assuming that I'm dumb and helpless. And I really don't like the thought that they're likely to treat people less capable of looking after themselves, such as my mum, in the same way.

I absolutely do not enjoy the judicial process. But I won't have these people getting away with being such bullies. So there.

And now I've got £2,775 to put towards paying off my tax credits repayment. Hah!

Hairdressers
10/11/2014

Continuing on this litigious theme -

I think you ought to be able to sue hairdressers. I blame my ex-hairdresser for my divorce.

Why would he want to make me look like a bloke?

In the Spring of 2008 he cut off all my hair without being asked to, and then told me that I would look like all the eventers I admire so much - like Zara Phillips, Mary King etc. Well if he had asked me whether to cut off all of my hair I would have screamed NO! NEVER!!!

Throughout my childhood my mother used to take me to the local (very cheap) barber for haircuts, and/or cut my fringe herself, really short.

Being an athletically built strong, tall sort of girl, the result was that everybody thought I was a very plain boy, and despite my best efforts, I never managed to become a teacher's pet. Clearly I have never quite recovered. I still really love it if a teacher actually likes me!

Anyway, every time since, whenever I have tried having short hair, it has ten times out of ten been an A1 catastrophic disaster! Yet this plonker went and did it, and charged me for the privilege.

Well guess what. Less than twelve months later I had no husband.

So I went to the head hairdresser at one of the biggest national chains, and asked him to sort me out.

"Whatever you do, don't give me layers, or I end up looking like Linda McCartney," I said.

So what did he do? Gave me layers. Without telling me. So I never realised that he had. And what did I look like? Well I can tell you that every morning I looked shorn, as the few long wispy bits of hair that he'd actually left seemed to disappear altogether.

Fast forward a few years; Ex has gone off, and I've got no money, so I gave up the luxury of a master hairdresser and risked a cheap salon in Tavistock instead. And guess what.

"We need to grow out these layers," she said. Well I'd wondered why my hair always looked so awful in the wind and in the mornings, and now I understood why.

And it's taken four years, FOUR YEARS!!! to grow out those stupid layers. That I'd forbidden the bloke to put in, in the first place! We finally achieved it last Wednesday. At last! Hurray! They say age is just a number. Well I think it's just a hairdresser. Thanks Charlotte! You have taken a decade off my 54 years!

Girlfriends Everywhere!
23/11/2014

My life is weird.

Last Friday I had dinner again with Malcolm and his new girlfriend.

The next day Will brought a girlfriend home for the weekend, and we were visited by Ex and his new girlfriend and her children for tea - on both the Saturday and the Sunday.

God, all this Love. What about me? I couldn't be working harder at finding it, but I'm getting absolutely bloody nowhere!

Meanwhile I had a lot of fun with Ex and his new little family. They are delightful. Two little girls who got on so very well with Faye that I begged them to stay and use the hot tub, while their Mum, Ex and I chatted together over a cup of tea.

Or was it.

Ex had made it for me and I couldn't tell whether it was tea or coffee.

And then I realised.

"I think you put coffee in it, and then forgot and added a teabag," I suggested.

"Would I do that?" he replied

"YES!!!!!" his girlfriend and I responded in unison.

Blocked?!!
23/11/2014

I have been 'blocked' again, by the only nice-looking bloke on Encounters. How very dare he?! I haven't even blocked a troll I've got called Piers, who has been genuinely rude to me, as well as boring - an even more heinous crime.

So I am racking my brains as to why this bloke, who calls himself 'ruth69er' or something, would do such a terrible thing. I liked the look of him a lot because he has a broad grin in every pic, doesn't use clichés, and comes from the same sort of background as mine. Well there's clearly something about me that he doesn't like at all. I suspect it's my great age.

I discovered this shocker as I was idly glancing at my iPad during a break from X-Factor - the programme's third airing in just one weekend!

Never mind. Another lonely heart has just popped up. This one says he's 6'3" tall and promises to provide the 'strength, excitement and charisma', to a new partner's 'loving, thought and care'. He is even prepared for this woman to be 'high maintenance'! Probably into S&M or something. No doubt we will find out. But he's put a zing back into my step after that rotten rejection!

Oh dear. The reply has pinged back. He's called Brian. The last two respondents prior to him were called Clive and Ron. At the risk of upsetting anyone reading this small tome, I'm afraid I just can't imagine spending the rest of my life with anyone with a name like that.

Mid-Life
24/11/2014

Mid-life crisis isn't just men throwing away everything they've built up over a couple of decades.

I've noticed some other behavioural traits.

For example, a lot of my mates seem to be moving house - I suppose before becoming too incapacitated to create a new and final community somewhere new for themselves for their dotage.

I've just returned from a two hour coffee break with Jilted Juliette who, like me, is also thinking about throwing in the towel and finally giving up trying to run the old family home all alone. She's had five years of living hand-to-mouth; providing her children with stability, seeing them through the nearby day-school, under constant threat of eviction; the poor woman never knowing quite how she is going to keep going, or what will happen next.

All this moving, though, is most annoying, as I'm running out of space in my address book, and it means I've got to make endless changes to my Christmas card list.

At the moment there are 418 people on my list (not that they've all remained friends, or are even necessarily still alive). I've got them on Microsoft Excel so that I can print off address labels instead of hand-writing all the envelopes.

Despite maximising efficiency, I still find sending out Christmas cards a time-wasting, expensive, pointless exercise.

Meanwhile receiving them is almost as bad.

Either you prop them up and they blow over if someone opens a door. Or, if you're like us, you staple them to a piece of ribbon, so that after you've lived in your house for twenty years, you've got twenty drawing-pin holes at the top of the wall above all your fireplaces and door frames.

And then, being paranoid, when Christmas is done you count them, to discover that you've been sent far fewer than you sent out; and then you throw them all away in huge black sacks.

Each year, whenever it snows, I race out with my pocket camera to capture a seasonal scene for next year's personalised card, so at least it carries some kind of news value. But yet again, this year - there's been no snow. So no romantic wintery scenes. What shall I do?

Another change that's happening, as we reach our 50s and our children are less dependent on us, is that we're freer to get out and about and catch up with old mates.

For instance, now that Faye's weekly boarding, I suddenly find myself in a position to play.

Every Thursday night I can do whatever I like! Weird! I haven't had a free evening since Ex exited. That's more than five years ago! I'm not used to this sort of freedom. How shall I use it?

Last Thursday I went to London for supper with my sister and three friends from my childhood. ("Were you a Victorian, Mummy?" asked Faye, who is studying the period at school.)

Since I last saw these three 'girls', I have been married and divorced. None of them ever even met my husband. One of them I mistook for her mother - she is the same age now as her mother was last time I saw her, and looks identical!

Then a few days later, my oldest, best friend of all, who lived literally next door for years as we were growing up, came over from Kent to stay the night.

Next Thursday is the ultimate treat. I'm joining a Blind Date from Encounters at the Races in Taunton, and then he's taking me out to dinner. What are the odds of this one proving a winner?

100 Potential Husbands
25/11/2014

Say I have now met getting on for 100 potential husbands through this internet dating lark.

Of them, 97 want a relationship with me, but I don't want one with them; and the only three that I like aren't interested in me. It's a long haul of a roller-coaster and isn't good for my sleep patterns, nor Cava consumption.

But I haven't given up yet.

And at the moment I am on a rather exciting 'up'!

There's Brummy 'Kodak', the one who's asked me to the races. In his picture he looks just like Malcolm.

Which is where any similarity ends. Malcolm reads the Guardian. Whereas this chap wrote 'bugger the planet' to me in his first email, and has a penchant for Range Rovers.

Having said that, he claims to do more than anyone to save the world, because his living is providing home insulation. I do so like a successful entrepreneur.

But I have never had a solvent partner in my life. I wonder how I would fair with somebody wealthy?

Also on my radar is somebody calling himself 'RunRabbitRun'. He's not very smiley in his pics, but is very good looking, so I think he might be hiding bad teeth.

He comes from East Sussex and has just sold his 30 acre smallholding after 20 years, so is in a similar place life-story-wise as I am. His son and daughter both had horses, so he knows one end from the other. His son's at Bournemouth University, and he's going to come and visit me.

Thirdly, there's Jago - very tall and good-looking, quite fun, and quite earnest in his correspondence. I think he's going to be disappointed by how not sweet I am. He's driving all the way from Harrow and back, to take me out to dinner at the best restaurant in the area, after I've had lunch with Peter, the good-looking bloke who drove me to the crooked garage, with whom nothing is ever quite going to happen.

Lastly is 'TreeHugger', who, despite his 'username', isn't a veggie leftie, but a Wykehamist academic who plants trees. He's really, really, really funny. Tall. Aged 58. He and I both have high hopes. But that first phone so often proves a killer. Fingers crossed!

As you can see, now that I have a little more time on my hands, I'm prepared to travel a little further afield in search of love.

And, on top of all that, tomorrow I'm meeting Little John from Taunton for the second time, during Faye's flute lesson. He's only 5'7" so I'll wear high heels to make him feel worse. Actually that's not the real reason. It's to make me look better. I met him through Guardian Soulmates when they had a special offer on. Even though his paper of choice is the Telegraph.

The AA says it's 6 minutes and 40 seconds from Faye's music lesson to the very nice hotel where we're getting together. Little John will buy me one Spritzer (for £9.30?!) and a packet of crisps. That leaves us with exactly 45 minutes and 40 seconds in which to drink and to chat. John is a charmer, asking all about me, and full of flattery. I can't get enough of that. Like a tyre with a puncture that needs constant inflating. Why is it that the short chaps are always so much nicer than the tall ones?

Tick Them Off
03/12/2014

Whenever I actually meet a date, it seems to mean that I can immediately tick him off my list. They just don't cut it in the flesh. So disappointing!

So Jago arrives, all the way from Harrow, in his mini cooper. He climbs out and he's nice and tall but oh no! He's wearing a white polo neck jumper!

Bye!

Less than a week later a convertible Porsche glides up the drive. Werrhay, result!!

In his blurb he said he was 5'11", so I'm in my stiletto's. I should have realised that if he was really 5'11" he would have put himself down as 6'.

I stride out to greet him, he emerges from his snazzy car, and his eyes are in line with my chest. He is a runner, lightly built, wiry. I weigh probably two stone more than him. He checks out of nearby Prince Hall Hotel the next morning without breakfast - even though he'd originally booked for two nights!

The only ones left now are Kodak and TreeHugger.

Treehugger's never been married nor got any children 'that he knows of'. But he says 'heck' as opposed to 'fuck', so I suspect ours isn't a match made in Heaven. I'll find out on Saturday anyway.

Kodak, on the other hand, seems to 'get' me. I asked him what he meant by referring to me as a 'proper bird', and he said: "Forthright, unique, articulate, fun, interesting. Many things but mostly wanting to be a woman, not wanting to be 'better than a man'. By laughing with us, not sneering at us."

Well, that had me walking on air for a day, but since I emailed him to ask him how much he weighs, he's gone quiet...

Skin
04/12/2014

'Will might have something useful for staying warm while riding in this hurricane,' I thought to myself, and pottered up the attic stairs to raid his drawers.

Sure enough - I pulled out a black and yellow slimy sort of garment made of plastic and put it on.

It slurped up my body so I could hardly move. I had to sort of peel it on, and its sleeves came right down, half-way along my hands.

I thought it must be something that they wear these days under their wetsuits for surfing.

But Faye advises me that it's called a 'skin' and accounts for the black bits you see on rugby players sticking out below their shorts.

It smells.

But. I say. We rode out on one of the wildest, bleakest, highest parts of the moor, somewhere beyond the Avon Dam towards something called Red Lake. No fun. And seriously cold. But I could tell that this garment was 100% windproof, while everybody else was chilled to the bone.

I think I must research a 'skin' made for a woman's shape, that fits, and doesn't smell. It was really, really good. I am so modern.

Broken
12/12/2014

I've got a broken nose, two broken arms and a broken foot.

All because of that stupid mad mare called Vegas. First it bonked me on the nose with its neck; then I knackered my arms grooming it, and then it jumped on top of my foot, which is now very fat with a purple imprint of a hoof across the top of it. If it doesn't stop hurting I might finally have to go to a doctor, but I can't imagine what they would do about it.

So in the meantime I have been flat out with hacking, dressage comps, swimming, lunching, hated Christmas cards, ensuring Faye wins her scholarship to her new school by forcing her to perform every night in every production the school puts on at the end of term for practice, selling my house, selling B&B nights, selling my holiday rental, and selling myself (to potential online dates).

I met TreeHugger last week, in the carpark at Keyhaven, outside Lymington. I commented how odd it felt to be back there 30 years later, after sailing there with an old boyfriend.

Well, small world. TreeHugger knew this boyfriend's brother, so together we went to visit their old holiday home. We found the house, left a note, and proceeded on our very merry way in the sunshine, to catch the ferry to Hurst Castle. We enjoyed a lovely walk back along the sand bank, and lunch outside (*outside,* in December!!!) on the roof terrace of a wonderful cafe in New Milton or somewhere, a little further along the coast.

TreeHugger says I'm like Downton's Dowager Countess, using something called 'aphorisms' all the time. This means, apparently, that I make weighty remarks based on zero evidence. Yup. Sounds about right.

Yesterday I hobbled out of the carpark at Taunton Races to meet my Brummy solar panel and insulation supplier. He's an ex-racehorse-owner. We have indulged in a very large number of laughs in our correspondence.

He sounds like the mirror image of me, even if he did leave state school aged 14 and live in Asia for a long time. And was married to the girl in the Special K ad. And now manufactures children's hand-sized pencils and pens. He only sleeps 5 hours a night and I found he was rather full on. I finally retired at the end of the day's racing exhausted by him!

It is a bit less effort with someone of your own ilk, so I'm driving all the way to Winchester tomorrow, to meet TreeHugger for the second time.

His messages make me laugh and laugh. He likes experimenting with 'Vibrant Purple' and 'Earthy Orange' in his emails, and we appear to have rather a lot of friends/acquaintances in common. OMG. What will he have heard about me from them?!

And then – assuming Peter-who-came-with-me-to-the-horrid-garage doesn't work out for me - I'm hoping he might be right for my mate Judith.

I will have a go at match-making them. So far he's my favourite date, and I would like to imagine them skiing happily together in Zermatt shortly.

So, today I'm thinking there's a lot of fun to be had with this internet dating bollocks, as well as the head-messing of it.

Getting to Sleep
18/12/2014

As I was nodding off, my head about to crash onto my desk, I thought I heard him say, "I could talk you to sleep.."

WHAT???!!!!!!!!!!!!!!!!

This was the charm offensive of some internet date calling me from Plymouth, whose 'username' I would give you if I could work out which one he was.

I had answered the phone with: "Is this NoButYesButNoButYesButYesButNo?". Well the answer was no.

Some time ago, "NoButYes" had blocked me when he had read in my blog that I once had a cigarette a decade ago - his no-compromise area.

But it wasn't NoButYes calling, and naturally enough the anonymous bloke at the end of the phone was a bit perplexed by my question. So he started going on about something else, and he really was talking me to sleep. No wonder he's still single!

Meanwhile Guardian Soulmates has sprung to life with two extremely erudite and articulate fans materialising within two minutes of one another, so I sent them the same reply, saying that I like the Daily Mail, X-Factor and Jeremy Clarkson. I am now massively frustrated that neither has got back to me as a result.

In the meantime, TreeHugger has become a very good friend - everyone will like him wherever he goes because he is clever, funny, and self-deprecating. He's also tall and very fit, eg he cycled 2012 miles around the UK in 2012 for charity. But it's not going to happen. He is properly hearty, whereas I will only use a portaloo if there are horses involved, and even then I will be grumbling all the way there and all the way back. And he punches me on the arm with enthusiasm, whereas I am supposed to be oozing mysterious sexuality, not being somebody's blokey mate.

So, meanwhile, you are allowed to think that I have become addicted to this internet dating lark and gone a bit mad. I would agree with you.

Encounters runs out tomorrow, and I only signed up to Guardian Soulmates because it was 50% off this week, meaning that just £16 could change my life forever!

I really, really, really would like to share my life with someone. But who that someone is going to be is proving most elusive!

Lonely This Christmas
23/12/2014

I turned down three offers of £2500 to rent out my house over New Year.

But got none for Christmas when it is free and empty. And then I discovered that my friend Helen, who is also a jilted wife and has a similar sort of place to mine, just outside Widecombe, turned down three offers of £2500 to rent out her house over Christmas, but would have been happy to vacate over New Year. We really must communicate more effectively.

My little family's Christmas was spent at my sister's new pile in Berkshire.

On Christmas Eve I limped in to Newbury's Mole Valley and Sainsbury, to buy last-minute stocking presents for the children, and then went on to A&E - the first moment in two weeks I've had to have my foot looked at, since Loony Vegas jumped on it nearly six weeks ago.

Row upon row upon row of empty chairs, and lots of signs saying 'queue this way' above empty echoing corridors. There was only one other person in the whole building. Interesting how nobody's ill when there's important shopping to be done. I sat for hours watching a special Christmas edition of Shrek until finally they took an X-ray, declared my foot 'fine', and sent me home advising me to stock up on Ibuprofen.

Meanwhile, having cleared the ha-ha of mowing cuttings, unwittingly dumped there over several years by my sister's 'polish couple', the rest of my extended family shared a delicious 'Cook' lunch together, and then all relaxed in the beautiful new drawing room, in front of a vast open fire, sipping coffee, listening to the Kings' College Carol Service - an eight foot proper Christmas tree bedecked with real candles as well as electric lights twinkling in the hallway behind them.

Because I was the only lone adult staying, I found myself sleeping at first on a mattress on the floor, and subsequently on one of the many sofa's, in order to avoid having to share a room with Faye and her night-long eczema scratching. Just think – if I had succeeded in finding myself a boyfriend, I would have qualified for a vast double bed in which we could have made mad passionate love all night. In total there were 14 extended family spread in various beds between eight bedrooms; leaving poor old me finally sprawled out on the sofa in the telly room.

I came into the kitchen on the first morning to find two husbands making tea to take up to their much loved wives. So I made myself an instant coffee and went back to my lonely sleeping bag.

Then that evening my sister was thoughtful enough to put a few things into a little stocking for me. Everyone was very kind and sensitive towards my plight.

A well-to-do Berkshire village provides a stark contrast to a mid-Dartmoor dysfunctional hamlet. On a beautiful frosty sunny Christmas morning we joined many others in the walk to the village church (actually I drove in the Golden Monster because of my squashed foot), to find it completely packed, almost entirely with people we had been at school with, or who our children were at school with.

Every Dad was in a tweed jacket or suit and tie. And the organist's day-job is assistant Head of Music at Eton College, so he was really rather good! Unlike the alcoholic who plays in the village down the road from Wydemeet, where you have to concentrate hard to recognise what carol the dirge he produces is meant to be.

I loved it all! Sometimes I would give my right arm to live somewhere where I am surrounded by people just like me!

Eat My Shit
02/01/2015

The lights on the plastic Christmas tree are flashing away as directed by their electric chip.

The fire is crackling in the grate.

And Faye and I are enjoying New Year's Eve, home alone.

"I wish we'd been invited to a party," she sighs wistfully, laying her pretty blonde head on my lap.

Two years ago I discovered that my South Hams gang - my best friends around here, or so I had hitherto believed - were all celebrating together, even including Ex and my children, having forgotten me, left rotting on top of the moor at home. Even though I'd emailed them prior to that hideous night, to see if they had any plans.

So instead I ventured up through the dark to the top of my lane, and popped my head through the door of the Forest Inn, but it was empty. A heavy metal band was playing stuff that I either didn't know, or else didn't recognise, and had clearly driven away anybody who wasn't already stone deaf.

In despair I retreated to Jools on the telly, and cried.

Well not this year.

"Perhaps we'll organise a party ourselves next time," I reply. "You can't expect people always to ask us out, if we never have parties of our own. Now. What would you like to eat most in the whole world for supper?"

"Packet macaroni cheese," is her all too predictable request. This will be the fourth night running.

Meanwhile I opt for Lidl's frozen De Lux Prawn and Scallop Cassoulet, and we settle down in companionable silence in the cosy sitting room to watch Chatty Man Alan Carr chatting nonsense from his sofa.

Except out of the blue, 12 year old Faye suddenly asks if we can turn to an award-winning arty film on BBC 2 about black home-helps in Mississippi in the 50s. As we watch, one of the servants serves her racist mistress a pie filled with human poo. Urgh. But this is art, so it must be a good thing. I am vastly impressed that my young daughter is so cultured.

Faye retires to bed when the film finishes, to get enough sleep to cope with tomorrow's New Year's Day hunt.

Alone once more, I ponder on the forthcoming year.

This time next year I might be relaxing in a new home with a new boyfriend, with a whole new social life based around Exeter, Faye's new school, and the health club. Both children will be boarding, so I will have oodles of time to waste. It could be a whole new chapter! Or possibly nothing will have changed at all.

And then I settle back very contentedly to see in 2015 with my old mate Jools as last year.

What a shame that the next day my tummy announces that I hadn't heated up the Cassoulet thoroughly enough.

New Year's Day Snog
03/01/2015

I am extremely proud and excited to announce that I have just enjoyed my first full throttle snog for a year! By which I mean for 365 days - not since 2014 which was a couple of days ago.

It was with a chap four years my junior, who sports a full head of blond hair. I came across him on Guardian Soulmates, and he has the same username as my horse - Vegas.

His daughter will be going to Will's school in September, and his best friend is my best friend's sister, dating back to when she and I were ten.

He popped by for tea, on his way to stay at Prince Hall Hotel up the road, and Faye went behind his head, gave me the thumbs up sign, and mouthed 'Yes!'

Blind dates cannot possibly stay here alone with me, B&B or no B&B, whether it's legal to ban them or not - I do hope I don't get sued for refusing their custom.

Anyway, after tea I slipped on my tightest LBD and high heels, and popped around to the hotel for dinner.

I was dead chuffed that after the most delicious and enjoyable meal, he started trying to snog me in the bar. But I just couldn't have that - not in front of so many of my friends' daughters who are the waitresses there - so I told him thank you, but no, and finally extricated myself after a rather jolly time.

The next day he emailed to say that he wasn't the right 'b-f' for me, which is a very kind way of putting it. I think what he actually meant was that now free after a very long marriage, he didn't want to get tied down to family life with an old bag like me, when he could be having fun with all sorts of people, and finally settle with someone ten years my junior!

Hey ho. On to the next one!

Second New Year Romance?
08/01/2015

Guardian Soulmates gave 50% off, and then Encounters offered me a free week's subscription. How is a serial online dater like me going to resist either? So of course I've taken up both and things have gone a bit potty again.

On Christmas Eve, five of the friends I've made through online dating emailed to wish me Happy Christmas, which made me feel slightly better about my lonely situation. I just wish I fancied one of them!

Then last week I met up with a chap calling himself 'Blueberry Man' at the Warren House Inn - the second highest pub in England - which happens to be equidistant between us.

I can usually tell who my blind date is the minute I set eyes on him. He will be looking up anxiously every time the door opens, and as I enter the room, a wave of recognition, relief and occasionally hopeful excitement lights up his eyes.

Meanwhile I think, "Another one bites the dust. Help me make it through the night."

Or, "How will I manage not to say something twattish that puts him off me?" or else, "I bet he thinks I'm too fat, old, wrinkly, opinionated and un-vulnerable," in the rare scenario of liking the look of him.

Blueberry Man's real name is Neil. Small world! He was once a client of mine! Back when we both lived in London and he worked for a company selling biro's.

We never actually met, but he knew my first boss who took me to the opera and asked me to be his mistress. When I refused, the old rake cheerfully remarked, "I suppose you still believe in all that love stuff."

These days I guess he'd be in prison for sexual molestation, but at the time I was charmed and flattered. For Christmas he used to give his female employees lacy black stay-up stockings. His navy three-piece pin-stripe suits were all bespoke and came with very tight trousers. He had a handle-bar moustache and was the drummer who banged out 'boom' at the start of "Waddya Want To Make Those Eyes At Me For?" He must be old and bent by now.

Blueberry Man told me how the nation's food is almost entirely produced by around just five companies - even the supermarket products that sound sort of home-made. Apparently the supplier/producer goes to one of these companies and tells them what he wants to make, then they manufacture the final product, package it, and distribute it in massive bulk. Small suppliers can only work with individual outlets and farm shops, said Neil, as they can't begin to supply either the quantities, nor the specialist expertise required in the manufacture of literally tons of product that the multiples require.

Our Dartmoor landlord was loudly crashing about, wanting us to leave, but we ignored him and continued a fascinating chat until closing time. Yet another good male friend made. But it's definitely not lurve.

One Day Too Late
08/01/2015

Did you ever stop to think that a scholarship to a private school can commonly be worth around £35,000? Thought not. But....

£35,000!!!!!!!!!!!!!!!!!!!!! Aghh!

That's more than most people earn in a year!

So, if you feel like getting your offspring privately educated (why would you? I still can't justify or explain it but hey ho), and your child stands the slightest chance of winning one, it would be crazy not to have a crack at going for it. I mean, really, how much effort would you put in, if you were pitching for a new client at work worth £35,000? Loads!

So of course poor Faye has been subjected to months and months of abuse, since I first thought of this, back in June last year.

I have put her in for an 'All Rounder' scholarship, which means she has to play two pieces of music on two instruments (or sing), recite a two minute 'monologue', perform music and drama with other contenders for twenty minutes each, take some special papers in english, maths and critical thought, and be interviewed by the head of music, the head of drama, and the head of school.

At the beginning of last term we took the major step of changing music teachers (because her existing one made her cry), and every week since then, I have been driving seventy miles each way for her flute lessons while I meet Little John, and last week we also did a 150 mile round trip in the opposite direction for an extra singing lesson.

We, and when I say 'we' I mean 'we', have prepared pieces on three instruments - two classical flute pieces, two musical theatre songs, and "Say Something I'm Giving Up On You", which Faye's done entirely on her own, singing mournfully and passionately as she accompanies herself on the piano.

And her english teacher has written a special monologue for her. It's Curley's wife from John Steinbeck's 'Of Mice and Men', being sad about the miserable life she leads, which Faye loves.

Faye's already practised her interviewing technique last year, when she applied for the head girl post at her current school, and in the forthcoming interviews she'll have to demonstrate all round massive enthusiasm and a wish to be a good role model in her new one. So let's pray that she's in a good mood when the day arrives!

"What will you give me if I get it?" she asked.

"Nothing. All the money I have gets spent on you already. There'll just be more for treats all around," I replied.

Rewarding children for doing well in exams, or bribing them not to smoke, is about as pointless as giving out surprise bonuses at work, in my opinion. You're either going to do your best at the job, or you're not. But hey ho. Nobody ever seems to agree with me on that one.

So anyway, even if she doesn't get the scholarship, the exercise of pursuing one has provided a focus, and Faye's musical ability has already improved beyond all recognition, so hurray whatever. On top of which, she's actually beginning to almost enjoy the process, and she really loves her new flute teacher.

I emailed the new school yesterday, to double-check whether they would like her to board overnight during the two-day auditioning process, and guess what they said. That I haven't sent in the application form and I have missed the deadline by a day.

I started shivering and my eyes filled. Oh my God. I've just found the form. Half-completed, lurking at the bottom of my pending tray. It's been sitting here since November, and we're now in January.

AAAAAAAAAAAGGGGGGGGGGGGGGGGGGGGHHHHHHHHHHHHHHHHH HHHHHHHHHHH!!!

"It's OK. Don't worry, that's fine. Just pop it in the post to us today," says Tania from Admissions.

Well now there's a big, fat, white envelope in tomorrow's post, with a completed form inside, and a massive first class stamp! Sometimes I could really shoot myself.

Next Husband
8/01/2015

Tonight I am meeting 'Dorset Man' who appears to tick every box. I am so excited that my hand is shaking as I attempt to apply my mascara. Having come across him through Encounters, it turns out that he is part of my childhood Dorset social circle!

I texted a great mate of mine, whose views I have immense respect for, saying "Potential blind date with thingy. Good or bad idea?"

And she texted back: "I think he's lovely. Colourful - both in attire and communication, and amusing."

Blimey! What else could you ask for? And he's 6'4" as well. I have spoken to him and he has an enormously attractive, friendly voice.

At last!

I am jittery.

I walk in through the door of 'Jack In The Green', and there he is right in front of me!

Um. Not sure what the problem is. Can't pin it down. We have friends in common right across England to a pub called The Bull in Ticehurst, East Sussex. But I'm not feeling it. Lots of mutual interest to discuss. He suggests I have a starter but he won't. He selects a delicious Rioja from the wine-list. A perfectly pleasant evening, and then the big shocker.

I am expected to go Dutch!!!!!!!!!! Well, dahling. It's been a long time since that happened to me. I have enjoyed all the nice, free meals I have been treated to over the past twelve months. Call me old fashioned. Sorry. That's curtains to a romance that never began.

Actually, I think to myself, I prefer 'my gypsy', tattoos and all. I met him, with no expectations, yesterday for lunch at the Double Locks - a delightful pub behind the Recycling Centre at the back of the Marsh Barton Trading Estate, on the bank of the Exeter Canal.

When I was at Exeter University 35 years ago, the pub was tiny, and had a goat and a parrot tethered outside. Now, in high summer, it has a marquee, adventure playground, bbq, 100s of benches dotted around its lawns etc. On winter weekday lunchtimes, though, it's silent and empty.

My gypsy's not much taller than I am. On the phone he sounded as though he smokes 60 a day and he sniffed like a coke-head, and didn't say anything very interesting. As I walked into the bar, he looked at me sidelong, and grinned.

He had an earring, sideburns, rings on his fingers and bracelets. He attended Barnstaple grammar and had S1's (that's the old S'levels which only unusually clever people even took) in maths, further maths, and applied maths, and a degree in psychology. He's currently negotiating to buy up a couple of film studios.

I liked his attitude towards me. Every time my wine glass was empty, he would jump up to refill it. And he insisted on paying the bill.

When the time came to say goodbye he hugged me hard and said he would very much like to see me again. But I had to extricate myself urgently because, as usual, I was deeply late for the school run.

Right now, having met up with too many dysfunctional public school types, I'm beginning to wonder how much damage a private education can wreak.

Life-Changed?
12/01/2015

Putting together your profile for this online dating lark forces you to reflect carefully on who you think you are, and what sort of a partner you are looking for.

I find that every time things go a bit wrong (ie every time I meet someone) I re-think the profile jobby.

This time, after my potential new husband disappointment, I returned home realising how much jolliness, and a spontaneous, infectious grin, matter to me.

I am also bored with feeling obliged to respond to messages from men who don't bother attempting to sell themselves to me, eg they send me a message saying 'Nice Profile'. Why would that make me want to marry them?

I have been unsure what to say, if anything, to Dorset Man.

So I was relieved to receive an email today which went:

"Marvellous to Meet You!

"But Virgo Meets Leo .."

Phew! (Although what was it about perfect me that didn't float his boat? And also, I am only half Virgo.)

I sent back a reply, copied and pasted from Google:

"Leo and Virgo
When Virgo and Leo join together in a love match, they may initially overlook common interests and feel they have nothing to gain from one another. This is a relationship that evolves over time. Leo is extroverted, dominant, and charismatic, and often has a short fuse. Virgo is studious and withdrawn, possessed of more versatility ...blah blah."

Spurred on by this disappointing encounter, combined with receiving a boring message accompanied by a photo of one of the most unattractive men I have ever seen in my life, I have just amended my profile.

I've added:

"You will make me laugh so hard that I do the nose trick down my front.

My car/truck is gold.

You wouldn't dream of describing yourself as 'an ordinary guy looking for a lady'.

Because you are as unusual, upbeat, and charismatic as I am. Or preferably more so! You understand and genuinely enjoy women, you have a spontaneous, contagious grin, and a knowing twinkle in your eye.

Send me a message saying 'nice profile' and I will reply because I am innately polite. Send me something more interesting with an attractive pic, and who knows - sparks might fly!"

Valentine Nightmare
02/02/2015

This year will be the first Valentine's Day I haven't received a card, since I was 11.

My other problem is - who to invite to Will's 'School Valentine's Ball'.

I wouldn't miss it for the world, as Will is playing the tenor sax in the Dance Band, while all the guests boogie together.

I've got no one to go with.

So my options are:

- take an internet dater. But it's Valentine's Night, and they will have to pay for themselves (£40), so they might get the wrong idea, and/or it doesn't seem fair to make them pay so much if they've got no involvement with the school; and Will may not like seeing me prancing around in front of his peer group with some weird-looking stranger with whom my relationship is unclear

- take my Mum (84) or Faye (12), but I would have to pay for them as well as myself, which is rather a lot

- find another Single Mum to come with me. Only a Mum involved with the school would be interested. I've found a really fun one, but she is still undecided.

So I've emailed the organisers who are the school's Music Department, explaining that I'm Billy No Mates, and might they put me on a table somewhere out of the way in the background?

Both Barrels
02/02/2015

I was so angry I turned Radio 2 up really loud, and drove off at ninety miles an hour.

Two days earlier I had enjoyed the best 30 minute internet-date phone chat that I'd had with anyone for a year. He had a lovely voice and made me laugh - a lot, even though he kept calling me 'Darling'. I identified with a huge amount of what he said, and our mutual acquaintance turned out to be the rather glamorous divorced Mum of Will's best mate, whose home is in Gibraltar.

His username was 'CliftonMan' and he had been pursuing me quite energetically via Encounters for a while, as initially I hadn't found him very inspiring and so hadn't responded to his messages with much enthusiasm. 'Let me be your Prince Charming' he had suggested. Pathetic.

Anyhow. Best chat for a year! The best one since Mr Dumped-Me-By-Email!

But then it transpired that in two days' time he was off to Gibraltar and away for three weeks! But first, he would be staying overnight in London with his children.

The very idea of "is he or isn't he 'the one'?" filling my head for over three weeks, filled me with dread. So I had a wizard wheeze. I could meet him for a coffee at the Services on the A303 opposite Hazelgrove School, as I drove back to Mum's from visiting Will's school in East Dorset, and as he drove back to Clifton from London via the A303 and the A37. The AA said this route would be 32 miles longer for him than going the normal M4 way.

Well. Would he Hell? He wouldn't even listen to my suggestion. He'd never heard of the A303(!) And then he accused me of being the sort of girl who is used to getting her own way (OK I usually do, but nicely.)

Then he told me that I am 'in a hurry for love' (OK I am, but in a pragmatic, un-needy sort of a way).

And then he referred to me as 'Sweetie-Mary'.

And he's very Anglo-Catholic, whatever that is, but it means he talks about God as if God were a Person. "God has a very good sense of humour, He loves laughing," this man informed me. Oh yeah? Who says? Is that in The Bible?

I stayed calm and friendly, until I received an email saying "YOU ARE QUITE LOVELY AND QUITE CONFUSED. I WISH YOU WELL" all in capitals for some reason. That was too much. How very dare he? It took me an hour and a half to compose my reply.

"I'm a Virgo mate - we are NEVER confused!" I ranted, and told him that I hadn't been made quite so angry for a very long time.

Being not listened to, and patronised, are not really my things.

I ended the rant by saying how interested I would be to meet him on his return, to see if we could laugh it off, or to find out whether we absolutely hated each other.

I don't suppose he'll reply, because I actually made myself sound a bit mad.

Hey ho. Back to Dutch 'Gerard' from the New Forest, and four Johns, two of whom I'm meeting this Wednesday, one for lunch and one for a drink later.

Clever Little Thing
06/02/2015

Fancy that!

She got it!

After ALL that, Faye has won an All Rounder Scholarship to her first school of choice!

I was surprised by my reaction. Not by the tears smeared all over my face, but because I suddenly realised that now she would just simply have to believe that she is special and talented. It's no longer just Mummy saying so.

And secondly her awe-inspiring Highly Revered Elder Brother (who is also an All Rounder Scholar) can now relax in the knowledge that his younger sister is not, after all, going around making herself look uncool all the time, and he can stop worrying about her.

Two out of two little scholars now, eh? I am feeling the most smug and complacent Mum ever, considering I'm a hopeless mother in most ways. I would advise everybody to keep away from me for the next couple of weeks, as I am enough to make anyone want to be sick!

See What Sticks
07/02/2015

My method of getting what I want is to throw everything at it, and see what sticks.

My top priority, as you know, is to sort myself out into a couple again.

Although I enjoy my own company very much indeed, I am definitely not happy on my own, long term.

To achieve this happy outcome I have:

- joined every website known to man or woman, favourited, messaged, tweaked profiles, photo's, met people, met more people, til I'm blue in the face, making bugger all progress, and now it's all ground to a halt

- arranged to promote myself on live telly via Channel 4's 'Four in a Bed' reality TV show a competition between B&Bs, if ever they're ready

- put my family home on the market so that I can get closer to Exeter, humanity, and the David Lloyd Health Centre which is full of eye candy

Desperate? Or pragmatic?

4 WILL IT NEVER END?

Valentine's Day
16/02/2015

I got three!

Sort of.

On the eve of Feb 13th, a red rose arrived from TreeHugger. He sent it by Interflora. Actually no he didn't. He sent it as an attachment to an email, rather cleverly done in 3D. Anyway - so that was a start.

In the post, on the actual day, came an actual card! It came from Little John, I'm sure - the chap I meet on Wednesdays while Faye has her flute lesson. He feels pure, like a breath of fresh air, after the many disappointed, complicated divorcees I typically meet through the websites. He's just a bit short.

And then on the morning of Feb 15th my mobile showed 'XX' - a Valentine text from another of the John's I'm in touch with.

Anyhow, so I'm feeling well chuffed.

After all that heart-searching about who should partner me to his School Valentine Ball, Will called to say he was ill. I've had to go and pick him up. I've been feeling pretty rough myself, recently. Lucky I seem to be a bit better today.

Yikes! So what is my poor divorced Mum-friend, who finally agreed to be my partner, supposed to do if I don't go? I bet she'll lose her bottle and duck out. That'll be two unused tickets. Bye bye £80!

Thought for the day: a disproportionate number of internet dates tell me that their wives have a drink problem, so they had to leave them. What drove them to drink, I often wonder. Does Ex describes me as a hopeless alcoholic with my daily £4.99 3/4 bottle of 11.5 per cent proof Tesco's Cava Brut habit?

Muddy Matches
20/02/2015

"The online dating and social networking community for country-minded, or 'muddy', people. This site is for anyone who leads a muddy-boots lifestyle and wants to meet like-minded, country people, be it for friendship, shared interests or dating."

I've been languishing on the Muddy Matches site for years - nobody ever contacts me. The only message I've ever received was from my mate Mad-Jack who is also on it, who dropped by through the ether to say what-ho.

Then jilted-wife Juliette emailed me to say the site was offering 'Free Messaging' during Valentine's Weekend.

So I 'signed in' and discovered that Muddy Matches has been telling its members that my subscription expired in February 2011. And the profile and pic are several years out of date. That explained quite a lot.

I updated my entry and spent the weekend sending out messages to anyone with two legs and a head.

The responses poured in. Well, dribbled.

Nonetheless, over the past few days I feel that I have been drowning in potential online dates. Only now, having spoken to a couple, do I feel that I am beginning to emerge out the other side.

Larry from Launceston shoots a lot. He doesn't realise that we have been in touch before. Nor that he had a chat with my mate Judith from Cheltenham, via Encounters. He calls, and sounds like one of those dissatisfied disappointed types. That's him done.

Then I speak to one of my many John's. It turns out that both he and Jeffrey Archer went to the wrong Wellington School - Somerset, not Berkshire. He sounds nervous of me. I can't be doing with that.

So now I'm left with Nick from Bude. He used to be an event rider. The thought of going hunting with a really good horseman fills me with excitement! He's coping with half-term at the moment, but we will meet next week.

Alistair runs a B&B just down the road from here, and is learning to play polo. His place has got rather poor reviews on TripAdvisor. "It needs a woman's touch," they carp. He's ideally after somebody who will give him babies, according to his profile, but I suspect he's missed the boat on that front. Certainly has with me. Anyhow, I shall return his call later today.

Another John, a back surgeon from Wales, wants to meet me next week, but he sounds rather a gloomy soul too.

And then there's..... Oh. My. God.

What's going on here then????

".... as one rocket scientist to another with no sense of humour at all I prefer you vastly to the many highly intelligent loggy firey sexy beach walkey cosy pubby make me laughey hags who have been invading me covered in debenhams jewellery... " (sic)

ChelseaChap is the first person for ages, on any site, who makes me titter.

He is currently holed up all alone in his family castle in Austria.

At last I am excited by this emailing dating lark - I'm even getting butterflies.

And then the bombshell.

He's famous! He's a living, breathing, proper, real film star!!!

Aagghhh!

There are pages and pages on him on Google - he even has a fan club!

And in 'images' he is so drop-dead-gorgeous-looking that I feel faint!

This is my come-uppance at last! I am no longer in control. He is wealthier, better looking, more successful and cleverer than I am. I am no longer in the driving seat! What do I do? I have never been in this position before! His ex-wife is far more beautiful and miles posher than I am (she is also first cousin to Malcolm, small world). I don't have any of the right clothes and I am much too wrinkly and fat for premieres. Heeeeeeeeeeeeeelp!!!

I am so glad that he and I have come across each other via the neutral, agenda-less, taboo world that is Online Dating. I would have been scared stiff of meeting this bloke at some dinner party or other.

He likes me! He responds with enthusiasm to my garbled messages!

Eek! I mustn't appear too keen. Can't reply again til this evening. Oh my, I am all of a jitter!

Ex-Mother-In-Law
20/02/2015

How grown-up am I?

Very. I've invited Ex's mum to stay.

And she is coming! Despite the fact that it's February! She would never have done that before, so she must really want this too!

She and I used to have loads of fun together before everything went wrong. We both liked doing the same things, like driving around Dartmoor, spending the day at Bovey Castle Hotel, going to hunt meets etc. And she was very good at wrapping stocking presents, and peeling, at Christmas times. I have missed her.

She arrived on a beautiful sunny afternoon in time to see Faye falling off during her jumping lesson.

Granny says she can't eat cheese, chocolate, alcohol or spices, so I find cooking for her very straightforward. School dinners. As I roasted the children, I mean chicken, I checked out the sitting room and there was Will playing Scrabble with her, in front of a roaring log fire. With her little dog curled up at their feet. I took a picture.

After a jolly dinner, including lots of puddings made from lemon, Main Item on the Agenda began. Boggle. I always win, no matter how much I drink or smoke during the games. I win by writing down the most, shortest words more quickly than anybody else - nothing particularly clever about it. Everyone was out to get me but it was fine. I won as usual.

How lovely, the next beautiful morning, for Granny to see both me and her elegant granddaughter at the hunt meet on our impressive hunters, amongst 94 other horses!

Fast forward, more Scrabble, more chicken, more lemon puddings, and more Boggle; in which Faye (12) beats Will (aged 16, and fifth top in his year at English), and Ex beats me!!!!!!!!!!!!!!!!!! Huh.

Craig
24/02/2015

"Hullooooo .... my .. name's ... Craig," he says in an unusual voice.

"God it's you. That is really bad acting!" I retort.

"Is that ... er ... Wyde .. meet?" he continues.

"You sound just like David Walliams!" I exclaim.

"Is ..er ... that .. Mary...?" he goes on.

"Urmmm, I suppose I am, " I finally answer.

"I'm ..er ... calling about the piano," explains Craig.

Oh no! I am mortified! I have been expecting Famous Film Star to call and knew he would be up to something like this. Instead, Craig the piano man has inadvertently impersonated my film star impersonating him. Agghh! I bluster, and backtrack, and blush to my greying roots which he can't see.

"You are quite bonkers, I am smiling all over my face," he reassures me.

This morning he rings again.

"Hullooooo .... my .. name's ... Craig," he begins.

"Oh hello Craig, how are you this morning?" I reply.

"I .. er.. want to book a room for my .. er.. honeymoon," he says. "I'm marrying him next Saturday..."

"Oh God it's you - I thought it was Craig impersonating you impersonating him..." and so my much awaited first call with Famous Film Star commences.

I have been so completely absorbed in fantasizing about him that I have become entirely distracted, forgetting things, unable to plan things, unable to concentrate, driving too fast with the music on too loud.

I am incredibly excited by all this - what on the face of it seems really to be like total fiction. I absolutely can't think about anything else. I have spent hours and hours giggling out loud to myself as I correspond with him via email. It will all turn out to be a complete waste of time, I am sure, but goodness how wonderful to be utterly buzzing at last. Everybody else I have met is grey next to this man.

We chat for 40 minutes. We have discussed so much via email already, and there is so much more ground to cover. I can't get enough of him. But he is finishing writing a play due to go on in the West End in the summer, so he is a pretty busy person. We might get together next week though. Can I wait that long?? So now I must make an appointment at the hairdressers, and buy some new clothes.

Depressed
08/03/2015

I am so depressed.

Nothing's interesting or fun. Nothing.

I haven't heard from him for 24 hours.

That means that he is acutely re-considering our lunch date, because he is frantically busy, doesn't want to put aside time for me on Thursday, and if I chase him up, regarding our meeting, then I will end up driving all the way to London for an embarrassing, expensive meal in Chelsea, that he doesn't actually want, and he'll be trying to hurry it up to get back to all his projects.

All is grey and bleak.

I sent him a jolly email this morning, and he hasn't replied.

My laptop is in the kitchen and every time I pass it, which is every five minutes, I press the refresh button, and all I get is yet another missive from some strange stalker on Encounters.

Lunchtime. OMG! Bingo! He writes: "Have you fallen off Dobbin?"

Hurray! Phew! He clearly didn't get this morning's message from me.

 I leave things a few hours, so as not to look too keen, and reply,

"So there I was worrying that you'd fallen under a bus."

Lunch is on! How exciting!

One Retailer vs Another
08/03/2015

I've got nothing to wear!

And it's all the fault of my favourite discount retailer.

Whenever I go there, I buy every black jumper and every pair of black trousers in stock that fit (I only ever wear black during the winter). I treat the shop as if it were a jumble sale, because everything is so cheap I don't bother to look at the price, and you're constantly fighting everybody else's elbows.

The mystery is, though, that if the garments really are top quality brands reduced by £100s, as they advertise, why do they seem to be such poor quality? Is it me?

When I get home, I wear the stuff, then put it in the washing machine on 'wool', and, whatever it is and however it started out, it looks like a rag at the end of the wash, and is many sizes smaller with no elasticity left; or alternatively the woolly jumpers have shed hairs all over everything else.

So to meet my sophisticated, to-die-for-good-looking Famous Film Star, in SW10, which is far smarter than SW6, I raced off to my preferred fully priced retail outlet, and bought shop-branded black jumpers and black trousers which were considerably more expensive, but which I hope will last through the wash.

I also ordered some new flat boots in case he is really short. He says he is 5'11" on his profile, but I bet he'll turn out just like that last one – a wiry little runner-type of about 5'10" at best.

My current flat boots have got holes in the sides where my bunions stick out, and are clearly in need of some proper cleaning, now they are five years old.

There is no getting away from it. My standards have slipped and I have become a Dartmoor Hillbilly. Even my haircut is rubbish, now that Charlotte has thrown in the towel, and somebody from the health club stole the only conditioner I have that works. I'm horribly badly dressed, wrinkly, overweight, and white; with two blobs of sparkly gold nail Shellac left on my big toes - the rest has fallen off.

My slatternly looks are all the fault of Faye's school merger.

In the olden days, when posh children went to her school, the Mums had their hair done in London and any carrier bags were Pinks, Hacketts, or Harrods. The new class of Mum (who is probably more friendly, and certainly more down to earth and relaxed) cuts her hair herself, is make-up free, wears an anorak and heavy flat shoes, and her carrier bags are Lidl.

So appearance-wise, I have mucked in and sunk to this level, and my urgent make-over is going to require some time and money. I'm never going to have achieved it by Thursday! Help!

Tennis Elbow
08/03/2015

I've got Tennis Elbow even though I haven't played tennis since I was thirteen.

It's pain in that ligament on the inside of your elbow. I've had it for months now, and it won't go away, however much I sit around doing nothing. It might be called Housewife's Elbow, but I'm no longer a wife, and my friend Sashka does nearly all my housework. It could be Riders Elbow - but Sashka does nearly all my grooming and mucking out too.

The other day, driving to see some old mates for lunch, I discovered what's causing it. It's Golden Monster Elbow. I've got the back of my truck's seat adjusted so that my arms are quite high and straight reaching out for the steering wheel. The problem is exacerbated when turning the wheel to park, if I'm tense. Which I was.

I was invited to a small party where I hadn't seen one of those attending since school - nearly forty years ago; and had never met his wife. I so wanted him to think I was still glamorous, as he was drop-dead gorgeous in his teens, and slightly scarily cool, arty and clever.

Well it was the most wonderful day, and my old friends made me believe I was still beautiful, funny and special. Oh, I feel quite wobbly writing this..

But I do think the drive made my arms feel funny.

And now the next trip is to London to meet up with the potential love of my life, and back home via friends in Bath. Oo-er Missus!

Thursday
10/03/2015

I put on my new black spray-on trousers, my 'best' old black jumper, and decided that I would prefer to have longer legs as a result of wearing heels and be taller than him, rather than being smaller than him, squat, in my ancient, holey old brown boots. Their new replacements failed to arrive in time. I topped the look off with my faux suede/fur moss green Betty Barclay jacket, bought in Peter Jones some time ago. It smells of mildew.

I arrived suffering from normal Golden Monster Elbow, to discover that I'd parked rather a long way from the restaurant. I put the one £1 coin I had in the meter, knowing it would only last ten minutes, and legged it to our eatery. He wasn't there, but as I turned round, I saw him outlined in the doorway.

He is an extremely youthful 63 - hardly any lines, not a hint of grey hair, very trim and relaxed in quality lambswool (possibly cashmere?) sweater and jeans. The very definition of what I would expect a successful actor of his generation to look like. And reassuringly taller than what I had feared - probably 5'10 1/2".

We arranged for me to move the car - he charmingly extracted 12 x £1 coins from the newsagent's next door; while I raced off to get the Golden Monster, hoping he was appreciating my long legs as I ran, meanwhile he stood saving an empty parking bay for me, right outside the restaurant's front door. While I was away his old mate Rory Bremner passed by for a quick chat; and then he was nearly run over by somebody who was determined to pinch the space. He was a bit shaken by the time I roared up in the truck.

Well. Four hours of non-stop chat and banter. He knows everybody and my goodness the tales. I cannot repeat them here. I would be sued! And he kept touching my arm because he is a touchy-feelie actor dahling. I nearly found myself instinctively reaching out for his hand! Eeek!

I would have liked to have stayed there forever, but had to whizz off through the sunny London rush-hour to get to Bath. As we hugged goodbye several times, both of us said, "Can I see you again?"

But, back in real life, surrounded by fog, drizzle, wind and sheep, on reflection, our lives have almost nothing in common.

If he lived around here we might be together all the time at one another's houses. Similarly if I lived in West London. But he is frantically busy with the most enormous amount of extremely high profile productions on TV, Edinburgh, and in the West End.

Meanwhile, I appear to be up to my neck in country pursuits and child-rearing. I never intended to be rural particularly. How did that happen?

And could I ever really become a luvvie? I'm not at all sure about that. I can't do the pink ones in Trivial Pursuit, and I never call anybody darling – not even my children.

I Hate Poldark
10/03/2015

Dark and brooding Poldark, beloved of Daily Mail readers, finally, after what seems like weeks, got shunted off page 3 back to page 5 today. Instead, on page 3, was a piece about how men don't like funny women.

Well I don't think Poldark's a bundle of laughs either, actually.

Imagine having dinner with him. How gloomy would that be? He wouldn't even taste the food. He'd just be gazing into his half-empty glass, being all sad and moralistic about his tin-mine, and you'd have to spend the evening trying to cheer him up. Exhausting. You would look over to that other jolly, laughing couple on the table next to yours, and wonder whether, however good-looking your date might be, you had really made the right choice.

But what annoys me most about Poldark is the series' stratospheric success.

Because since it all went ballistic my Famous Film Star, who is in it, hasn't got time nor inclination to send me long hilarious emails anymore.

His world has gone potty and is much too frantic to include little old Dartmoor Hillbilly me. He is now made, his future assured, because of the success of stupid Poldark.

There are another ten books left to film for God's sake! Years and years of the stupid programme! Whereas if it had been a disaster there wouldn't be another series, the media wouldn't have gone mad about everyone in the cast, and my film star might have had time to think about coming to visit me here on Dartmoor.

I'm Joining The Gym
11/03/2015

Apparently, these days, the most common place for relationships to start, after the workplace, is in the gym. I heard it on Radio 2 last week, so it must be true.

Hellooooo, David Lloyd!

The Exeter David Lloyd Health Club simply breathes beautiful, classy, healthy-looking people. As well as being opposite the Exeter Chiefs' ground at Sandy Park. I want to become a part of that scene, so I've joined. I don't care how much it costs. A lot, as it happens. About double the monthly cost of Encounters. Let's hope their gym proves more effective at matchmaking!

Urban or Rural?
12/03/2015

Muddy Matches asks you to say in your profile what percentage urban vs rural you are.

When I was first a subscriber I put that I was 90% rural because I thought I would get more 'fans' that way.

But actually I don't know what I am, and recent events have underlined this dilemma.

Famous Film Star has gone cold. Boo hoo. I reminded him that I am visiting London for a dinner organised termly by Ex for London based parents of children in Will's school year. And this time I'm included too, even though I live 180 miles away.

The dinner is to be held a short Boris-bike ride from Famous Film Star's home. But he is too busy with Poldark and everything else to see me. I am not quite gutted, but it's a bit of a bummer.

A couple of days ago, when I was hacking home on my horse, Perfect Panda, a lone, young, male foot-follower wound down his car-window and, smiling warmly, asked me if I had far to go.

I have noticed him being around and about before. He is so rural that he wears walking gaiters. I did a bit of research and discovered his page on Facebook. He is 'passionate about hunting, shooting, and fishing'. He's the sort who has an on-going subscription to the Countryside Alliance and yomps for fun across the moors. Whereas I would rather relax in my hot tub with its flashing fluorescent lights.

The Book's Done!
17/03/2015

I'm still in my pyjamas.

It's 5.45pm.

I wonder what the Tesco delivery man thought when he arrived here just now?

But it's done! The first draft of my first book is complete!

I have ordered a couple of memory sticks and will pop it onto those and send it to some friends for checking, tomorrow.

Meanwhile I shall investigate self-publishing options and report back.

Perhaps all the publicity my marketing of it will generate might even help me sell Wydemeet, and find a boyfriend! I'm going to turn myself into a celebrity author!

Tiny Tims
17/03/2015

There are currently five intelligent, articulate Dates who are interested in me.

All five are under 5'9", two are called Tim, and two are called Richard. Or, to be more precise, one is called Dick.

"You're not really called 'Dick' are you?????????????" I wrote back. So now I'm calling him Richard in order to take him a bit seriously. And the fifth one is my old mate Little John.

It's a bit of a bugger, sometimes, being tall. I'm really not at all sure I could fancy anybody as little as these guys are. I expect that's why they've ended up on an Online Dating site. A bit mean of God, this, don't you think? To be so Height-ist?

Direct to the Top
20/03/2015

Nobody ever wanted to sit next to the company chairman at Christmas office parties.

Except me.

So, as the newest, most junior executive in the PR firm - I was the only one to volunteer for the position. And what was the result?

"Do you want to hear all about what really goes on in your company?" I whisper to him, over our flaccid turkey.

Of course he does. So I tell him, and the result is that I am well paid, quickly promoted, and remain great friends with him to this day.

So my policy is always to go directly to the top.

When our McVitie's Penguin Polar Relay team of 25 jubilant women returned triumphant from their expedition to the North Pole, back in 1997, I called Tony Blair's new office at No 10 and invited us all to tea.

And now I've gone and done it again.

I've asked the new headmaster of my daughter's merged school, and his family, for Sunday lunch. But not content with that, I've also invited the new vice headmaster and his family, and two other families, that I don't know all that well either, who I like a lot because they are 'do-ers'.

I'm not quite sure anymore why I've done it. I've chosen a day when Ex is here to help. One of the families was extremely kind to me all day last Saturday, when Mad Vegas went potty at their hunt meet. And the other family has been very hospitable to Faye and me over the past few months.

I'm wondering to myself whether I have a hidden agenda, but if I did - I've forgotten what it was!

Solventandfun
01/07/2015

He's wearing round glasses, a flat cap, a tie, and tweeds, in the picture, and has a very happy grin.

I 'message' him saying, "I bet we've got some friends in common," and it turns out that we have. My estate agent for a start, who's currently attempting to sell Wydemeet for me.

My new date says how nice it is to hear from me. "It makes a pleasant change from unemployed 60 year old back ends of a bus from tenements in Glasgow, who seem to think that I might be the answer to their problems," he remarks, adding that his children refer to him as 'Posho', and that the uniform he has to wear to chauffeur his wealthy clients around in, and assist them on shooting parties in, is very expensive.

We meet 'halfway' in Bath - my suggestion - which turns out to be 2 1/2 hours of travelling for me, and 45 minutes for him. But he's worth it. Except that I'm the rower, and he's the cox. I must weigh twice as much as he does. And I am clearly older. We look faintly ridiculous together. This is never going to work.

On to the next one. Lunch today with 'Neutron', in a very trendy-sounding fish restaurant in Topsham, where one review comments that you would expect more than paper napkins for the prices charged. I hope he doesn't make me go dutch!

He's also 5'10" but describes himself as 'stocky', so hopefully he'll weigh more than me.

Lunch with Ex-Con
02/07/2015

At dead of night, the putt-putt boats would cross the sea to a beach in southern Spain, the marijuana was taken ashore and transported up the mountain by donkeys, and subsequently distributed around Europe by miscellaneous university undergraduates and students on their gap-years.

Neutron, the brains behind the arrangement, did three years inside for his pains.

"Today's weed is still OK," he advises me, "but don't touch skunk, and definitely don't try those new legal highs."

All highly useful expert info for a mother of two teenagers, now it's 2015.

Our restaurant has described itself as an 'upscale scruffy-chic dining room with exposed brick walls', and the starter is Pan Seared Scallops, Warm Black Pudding, Pea Purée, Confit Leek, Asparagus, Pea & Dressed Pea Shoot Salad. God it's good.

I bet the people serving us would be surprised if they knew that my luncheon partner's an ex-con. Tears trickle down the sides of his face as he describes the recent agonising slow death of his partner of twenty years, the most intelligent woman he has ever met - he tells me - as she became increasingly hospital bound and institutionalised, and then was finally gone.

These days he travels around Europe in a camper-van, going anywhere, anytime he likes, limping. He's got a hole in his heel, he explains. The result of an infection acquired in France.

Such a life has certain allure. But I think I'd rather stay at home.

I Hate (Giving) Presents
15/07/2015

Although I don't mind receiving them!

It's just that they're such a hassle, providing something that people would already have bought for themselves if they really wanted it (with the possible exception of Jo Malone bath oil at £50+ a bottle).

Going through the divorce finances lists six years ago, I realised that 'presents' needed an entire column to itself, they're so expensive. And that's just me - who's selfish and mean. How on earth much do normal, generous, kind people spend a year on gifts?

I tend to present people who must be thanked, with soaps and room fresheners from TK Maxx, wrapped in reduced priced paper, or stuffed into those pretty little paper bags that someone gave to me first.

Nice people bring me large bunches of fresh flowers encased in designer-brown paper and ribbons, hand-made chocolates that aren't past their sell-by date, and bottles of wine with corks in as opposed to metal caps.

So for me, the worst part of Faye leaving the school which I've loved for nine years, has been the dilemma over what presents to give the teachers.

The thought of distributing 25 bottles of expensive, or even relatively cheap wine, which will be forgotten in a couple of weeks, fills me with horror.

So - hello eBay, and there they are. Mugs, mugs, mugs, mugs, mugs. All with "Number 1 Teacher" written on them.

My current B&B guests are teachers, so I interrogate them as to how I should play things.

"Anything but mugs," says Ronald. "A heartfelt letter is best. I've only ever received two in twenty-five years of teaching, and I've kept them both," he adds.

So. Twenty-five heartfelt letters is going to keep Faye busy this Sunday.

Back to eBay and here we are!

Two mixed packs of 'thank you' cards (20p each). Personalised hammers ("Mr ? Thank you for helping build my life") for the man-teachers; and hand-painted wine glasses for the lady-teachers. And lastly a little bench inscribed "With thanks from the Hadow Family 2015" for the rounders field where there was never anywhere for me to sit.

Still expensive.

Telephone Man
15/07/2015

My radiant, blonde, innocent, thirteen year old daughter is grinning from ear to ear at the assembled teachers, schoolchildren and their parents, as she does something rather rude with the hand of the science lab's skeleton hanging from his hook, an official-looking blue cap perched on his skull.

"Now when other fellas call ya tell 'em how it all began" she slurs, in a broad southern-American drawl.

Yikes! I had no idea how rude those words really are! Hopefully most of the audience won't get what she's actually on about.

Then she changes the mood completely.

"Say something, I think I'm losing you..." she sings her favourite, with sweet melancholy and total lack of self-consciousness, gazing into the middle distance, as she plays the sad chords on the school's grand piano.

It's the 'Leavers Concert', where anything goes, and the first opportunity that Faye has ever really had to publicly show off her talent. If you knew how ridiculously proud of her I am, it might make you vom.

Big choking and swallowing and wet eyes follow the next afternoon, when she wins an obscure plastic little cup that she's allowed to take home as it will probably never be awarded again, because the school is rationalising its cup collection post-merger. It's called the 'Community Cup' and it's awarded to the pupil who brings 'the most happiness to others'.

"I've never won a cup before, and today I've won four!" cries Faye to the many friends crowding around her. I take a picture on my phone of her clutching them all - cups for Music, Drama, and a huge silver 'House Cup'.

But it's the plastic little fourth one that means the most to her Mum and her Dad.

Six Men Become Five
30/07/2015

I have been getting myself into a bit of a muddle.

Here I am, on a week's cheap holiday with the horses in The New Forest, while Wydemeet is rented out.

Only it's not turning out to be that much of a holiday. I had been worrying that I might be a bit lonely out here in wildest Hampshire, so I emailed some old mates who live here, and things have started to go a bit mad.

Now it looks as though I'm going to end up seeing six different men in seven days! And that's on top of visits from Will and from my mother.

First I emailed Elias, who is an old boyfriend from when I was eleven. Well he was hardly a boyfriend actually. Just someone that I was totally, madly, passionately, blindly in love with. Or probably more accurately, infatuated with. He's 63 now, happily married for 19 years, with four children. I hadn't seen him since his wedding day and had never met his wife except then. He replied straight back to my email, inviting me to call him to make a plan.

Then I emailed Chris, my great mate from school.

I emailed TreeHugger.

I was contacted by some bloke on Encounters calling himself Que Sera Sera, determined to book himself into my hotel and buy me dinner.

Next there's a tentative dinner planned halfway between Weymouth and the Forest with my great online mate-date, Peter.

And now - God knows what the hotel thinks - but at 9.30pm this evening, some man that I've been on the phone to regarding a possible change of livery for my horses, has come into reception and rung up to my room, inviting me to join him in the bar! I said sorry, but I'm heading towards bed (which isn't true, and it's the only lie I've told all year). So I hope he's gone away. How intriguing though!

My day with Elias proved extraordinary and I doubt I will ever forget it. I called him on the second morning of this so-called holiday, bleating on about how unhappy I was with the horses' livery that I had booked.

"Bring them here - we've got five!" he said. Funny - I thought he was a yachtsman, but hey ho.

"This afternoon I need to hand Faye over to Granny, fifty miles in the opposite direction from you, at Dorchester's McDonald's," I countered.

"Not to worry - I'll organise my driver to take her," he swatted away my next concern. "I've booked lunch for four - you, me, and the boys. Do come," he continued. "The girls are at a horse competition."

So Faye and I packed up the horses, attached the trailer, and pottered off to Elias' house - the same one in which he celebrated his wedding day all those years ago - and life suddenly became sunny.

Faye was then whisked off to McDonald's in a shiny chauffeured Jag; while Elias, his two sons and I leaped into a fortnight old, four-door Aston Martin, to enjoy confit shoulder of lamb and a rather pleasurable little Right Bank Bordeaux, at the best hotel in the Forest.

The following day, Chris and his lovely wife Carly took me to the Members' Enclosure at the New Forest Show, and drowned me in so much exquisite English champagne that I felt loved and happy, and a bit like a queen.

TreeHugger came to my rescue next. Very familiar with the moor, having spent most of his early life there, he was determined to find a proper livery for the two horses. And after considerable trouble he succeeded. It's located an hour away at the opposite end of the Forest from Elias' house - but oh my! What a place for riding! And on top of that TreeHugger insisted on buying me dinner.

Fifth was Que Sera Sera. He appeared, freshly showered, walking down the hotel stairs as I crashed through the hotel's front door, returning late from riding, with 'hat hair', four day sweaty old favourite riding top, horsey jodhpurs, and ill-matching socks. It was obviously him - you can tell these blind dates immediately. Pale blue shirt, jeans, and 'wide' shoes, by which I actually mean very narrow, if you get my drift. There's no way that he's 5'10" as advertised, but he's stocky, and obviously weighs more than I do which is the main thing.

He's got a big nose and wide mouth, and might be of Jewish rag-trade origins. I daren't ask him, in case he isn't.

The funny thing about this meeting is that although he's about as far removed from my correct, private-school-educated world as you can get (and we mutually roared with laughter when I told him that I went to school at Eton), he has a presence about him that I like. He's done a lot of things including being an international debt collector. I have a feeling that his Birmingham mafia connections might even re-arrange my errant ex-plumber's face, were I minded to ask them to.

If I introduced him to my Mum, she would possibly be horrified. Or she might warm to his charm. I'll have to think about that one.

So I ask my best mate Judith to hack into my Encounters site to see what she makes of Que Sera Sera.

"Ha ha! I know him!" she emails right back.

There's no mobile signal and the hotel phone costs £2,000 a minute. Agh! This is just too intriguing! I'm going to have to retire to bed (Que Sera Sera has gone back to his own room) in a lather of exasperation, not knowing anything more! Where on God's earth would posh Judith from Cheltenham have come across this wide-boy from Birmingham??

Which just leaves Peter. Dinner halfway to Weymouth on the last night of my mini-break. But he's just emailed to say that he can't make it as he's suffering from something called a hiatus hernia. Just five men in seven days then.

Nice Date
19/08/2015

I met an internet date that I liked yesterday. That makes a nice change.

He's called John (as so often), and he's got a tattoo. In fact - more than one! I've never knowingly ever had lunch before with somebody with tattoos.

But he also knows how to pronounce Ascot, and he's friends with the only family to have had more boys at Harrow than any other - ahead only of Ex's family.

If he hadn't told me, I might have guessed he'd been a rugby prop - from his body-shape, his ears, and his teeth. But he did tell me, so everything fell into place.

I think you're beginning to gather that I quite like these stocky blokes who may be shorter than I am, but weigh (even) more and are very strong - hopefully mentally as well as physically.

Like me, this bloke's a networker - he knows more people than you could ever imagine, from all walks of life. He's one of those shaven bald-headed people - nothing like anyone from my normal background.

But I do like individual, and I do like entrepreneurial, and I would have enjoyed spending even longer with him, sitting in the warm sunshine at the Double Locks, while Twiglet attempted to wage war on the rather large cygnets.

Modern Mature Relationships
20/08/2015

I'm thinking that I never want to share a house with anybody ever again.

I'm thinking that sharing your home with a spouse is a good idea if you have children, but after that it's probably a bit rubbish.

I'm daydreaming about some Adonis coming to stay with me for a couple of nights at a time in the new romantic forest glade I have my eye on, with its herd of wild deer popping their heads through the french windows of my new bedroom, as the sun rises behind them.

He would be my treasured guest and I would look forward to his arrival and, when he pulled up in the drive I would stop whatever I was doing to run out to greet him, with a huge grin, and an iced G&T.

I would cook properly for him, and talk to him over supper, instead of watching telly.

With him staying at my house, I could still stack my dishwasher as I like it, and store the leftovers on their correct shelf in the fridge. If he left the loo seat up once or twice, it wouldn't drive me nuts.

A few days later, I could make a return visit to his place, where he would make me feel like a queen.

This way, there would always be an escape route.

Toy Boy
05/09/2015

Fancy that.

I've been 'favourited' by a bloke aged 42!

He's after a 'glamorous tomboy'. Hah! I like that! That's me! Why didn't I think of describing myself like that? I add the expression to my profile, and return to 'Clerkenwellkid'.

"Och aye the noo and foo's yer doo's" I write to him. No idea what it means, but also on his profile there's a picture of him wearing a kilt, jumping through the air across the roofs between two buildings. He looks mad, and very smiley. I like that too.

Anyhow, he turns out to be called Jack, not Brian or Dave or Ron or anything, and then, blow me down with a feather, as I'm talking to him while he's in the bath, it turns out he was educated at Harrow! Where Ex went! And half my family!

Only of course because he's 13 years younger than I am, we know no one in common. Ooops. I wonder whether he listens to Radio 1? He could go out with someone in their 30s! What will he think about my crepey old skin!

I have found that my complexion has improved with the regular use of Boots Protect and Perfect serum, but no way do I look like someone young enough to have children.

I'm picking him up from Tiverton station on September 20th. How on earth is this one going to go?

Wombat25
09/09/2015

The sooner my subscription to Encounters runs out the better. I'm utterly fed up with this online dating thing. Only a couple of days left!

My final two 'live prospects' are now 'Clerkenwellkid' and 'Wombat25'.

Clerkenwellkid, as we know, is a 42 year old Old Harrovian. Wombat25 turns out to be a 66 year old Old Etonian (who I am rather taken by. He is very chatty and says I sound 'heavenly'. Also, he knew my Dad, who taught there. I wonder how ancient and wrinkly this bloke is?)

Anyhow. How mad is that? And why can't anybody be in their 50s?

How long is this endless, fruitless quest to continue?

I can't wait to find out!

So after I've met the posh blokes, I'm going to be bombarded with suitors as a result of Mary Hadow Awareness Month: newspaper article in the Saturday Telegraph Supplement about selling my home, 'Four In A Bed' B&B reality TV show on Channel 4, and launch of my first ever book - all happening over the next couple of weeks.

What on earth will I be writing on here by the end of this month?!

Old Harrovian ToyBoy and Old Etonian Pensioner
21/09/2015

Clerkenwellkid was supposed to come and visit me yesterday.

I had heard nothing from him since it was all arranged, so texted him a couple of days ago. But of course this being on my stupid new phone, despite the thing being advertised as coming complete with some app-thing named "EE Wifi Calling", the text didn't get sent. So on the day of his planned arrival, between preparing fried eggs and scrambled for my B&B guests, I traipsed out into the rain in my wellies, halfway up the field, where there's a signal, and re-sent the text, while Mad Vegas the horse entered stage left and attacked me. Clerkenwellkid texted back saying he was coming!

And that is the last I have heard.

Meanwhile, after a two week silence, Wombat65 contacted me out of the blue via Encounters last night, saying that he hadn't forgotten me and would be watching TV at 5pm this evening, when the first of five episodes featuring me on Channel 4 goes live. He's obviously been waiting to see if I am good enough for him. I'm not sure how much I like that.

Bye Bye Wombat65
21/09/2015

So it's a 'non' from the (very) Old Etonian (66).

Within half an hour of checking me out on telly.

Unkind.

Amusing
07/10/2015

I hate the word amusing.

And humorous.

And LOL.

And GSOH.

All are palpable proof that their writer is just not funny at all.

CV Video
11/10/2015

My Four In A Bed project has had an unexpected side-effect.

It comprises a kind of video-CV, so that I can direct any potential suitors from Encounters towards it, to check me out on catch-up.

Having been so inconsiderate and rude by not turning up, nor returning any urgent calls nor texts a couple of weeks ago, Clerkenwellkid contacted me again and I suggested he look at the Denouement episode before we went any further.

Well, having watched it at 1.30am this morning, he got straight back to me saying he thought I was 'fab and gorgeous'!! So that's a bit better than OE Pensioner's response, and has cheered me up no end!

Three further potential dates: Request123, RugbyBoy and Chrisnat are all also on my case, having tuned in. So I can't be as unattractively bonkers as I had imagined, having watched the programme for myself. I am lying in bed this morning, typing this up, grinning from ear to ear!

Dumped-By-Email Pops Up Again!
11/10/2015

"You are very welcome to take off your shoes," said Claire, our class leader from the Totnes branch of the National Childbirth Trust.

Several Mums-to-be disposed of their Conker Cornish pasty shoes and crossed their floral-clad legs as a slight smell of joss-sticks, weed and vegetarian cooking wafted about them. The remaining three remained steadfastly fully clad sitting upright, as we had all been taught to do from an early age at our private schools.

Seventeen years later, we three all meet again, at a talk for parents, over a cup of coffee in the foyer of Faye's new school. After all this time, we are suddenly now all school parents together!

A very friendly and smiley old girlfriend of Ex's from thirty years ago, whom I haven't seen since our wedding, comes over to join us.

And then suddenly - hello! Oh My God! Suddenly appearing by my side is Mr Dumped-Me-By-Email!! He has two boys at Faye's new school.

His appearance is only slightly less good-looking than I remember. He's still wearing exactly the same clothes, right down to his clog-things. But what I liked most about him, all that time ago, is still there. He is entirely natural, smiley, and easy to be with. This encounter is so, surprisingly, not embarrassing.

As the other Mums gather around to gently flirt with him, we all move into the main hall for the talk, and both the head and the vice-head come over to sit next to him, me on his other side. It feels nice, warm and comfortable to sit next to a bloke you've known for a while, in front of everybody, like this. I am so pleased he appears so easy about it.

After all, he is quite a lot responsible for my even thinking of sending Faye to this fabulous, perfect school where after less than six weeks, she is already so very happy.

Mellee
11/10/2015

I have been missing the weekly glass of wine I used to share with Little John during Faye's flute lessons.

Ex-Guardian-Soulmates Little John and I must have known each other for a year now. He is such a charming person and always makes me feel happy, snug, warm and tingly.

Well he's missed our sessions too, and has invited me out for a belated birthday lunch prior to The Rugby Match between my daughter's and son's schools. He even brings me flowers!

Over a delicious meal of pork belly, and rhubarb panna cotta in our nearby posh country-house hotel, he is as charming and chatty as ever, and then we move on to the touchline of Faye's school's FIrst XV rugby pitch.

This is surreal.

Faye's school is playing Will's school.

There on the pitch is my absolutely totally beloved only son, looking utterly gorgeous, concentrating hard, and slightly nervous. But playing at Faye's school! Too weird!

On my right is Little John, who has never met Will, dapper and neat amongst this unfamiliar bevy of shouting, anxious parents.

Ex suddenly appears at my side, having driven 150 miles from London to catch this important match, pacing backwards and forwards as Will's school's Number 10 refuses ever to pass the ball to Our Son.

To my left is our adored daughter, and four other Year 9s, one who also has a big brother playing. They have formed a little line of brightly-coloured, blonde-haired cheerleader-groupies. One of their mothers, who is even older than I am, rushes up to congratulate me, having recently 'caught up' with my telly appearance.

And then suddenly, up from behind, appears Mr Dumped-Me-By-Email, grinning broadly.

"My brother called me to say, 'I think there's someone on TV that you ought to be watching'," he laughs. "And suddenly there on camera was one of the participants trying on my ex-wife's ski jacket that I gave you!"

Mr Dumped-Me-By-Email turns back to the rugby, and Little John pops back up.

"You're much the most stylish mother on this touchline," he stands on tiptoe and whispers in my ear.

TopChef
04/11/2015

Oh no! Not shiny, light tan, narrow, pointed, lace-up shoes again!

Shall we bother with lunch?

Deary me. Why am I such a bigot? The only person who suffers as a result of this affliction is me. But I really don't think I could go out long term with somebody who wears shoes like that.

TopChef is waiting for me in the cafe of my health club. He first contacted me via Encounters and when I directed him towards my potted 'Four In A Bed' CV he recognised me as having grinned at him one day as I emerged from the pool.

Online he describes himself as 'an honest, ordinary bloke'. Well bloody hell, call me contrary, but I would rather have a liar! I 'messaged' him back saying, "I'm not optimistic that this will come to anything as I am far from ordinary. But it would be nice to have a mate at the health club."

So here we are and all is just as I thought. He's an ordinary looking very decent, friendly bloke, and insists on paying for my lunch, which is always appreciated. I have my normal 175ml glass of Sauvignon while he has a cup of tea. He has never eaten at the health club before in three years. Eh?!

Every Monday and Friday (which are my days too) he does something called 'Spinning' which involves riding a static cycle to music. He says there are a couple of fat women in his class who sometimes fall off. According to your fitness levels you can change gears so that everybody can easily stay in time.

I said, "Did you cycle from home to the club then?" That might have been more productive in saving the planet kind of thing.

He left after no more than an hour of my scintillating company, in a hurry to get back to work.

Grotty Potty Yachtie
15/11/2015

He's blown me out again.

How dare he?

He's only 5'9", went to a secondary modern in the north and then headed up a printing company, and now he claims to run a racing yacht brokerage, yet he hasn't heard of Dubois Yachts, who are probably the most highly respected specialists in race-yacht design in the world. I know all of this because his name is Ifor, and I checked him out on Google. There is nowhere to hide these days. Also there is an old picture on Google, of him looking completely awful with a stupid sort of beard.

And he spells definitely definately.

The challenge is how to deal with these people who don't even realise they're born.

I could text him back and say, "Once you've finished meeting needy, bitter, neurotic alcoholics who tell you they are younger and thinner than I am, but aren't, perhaps you might deign to join me for lunch or dinner when you are guaranteed to leave entertained, if nothing else." But I'm not going to do that - it sounds too ranty and begging. I have learned over the years that the most effective way of dealing with these people is simply not to reply at all, so I'm not.

Vanilla
27/11/2015

As you know, one of the key reasons I took part in the telly thing was to see why I have never had a queue of men falling on their knees at my feet.

I have decided that this is because most men prefer vanilla women. Who are gentle, sweet, kind, serene and calm. Who don't make waves, or query the bullshit. Instead, uncomplaining, they cook lovely Nigella meals using fresh ingredients from M&S.

What would you be if you were a herb, or a spice, or a bit of food?

I would not be a chilli - I am not fiery enough. Nor ginger. Perhaps coriander or tarragon? They have a bit of a bounce. But I am too unusual.

I have decided I would be a truffle. Rare, valuable, earthy, and not to everybody's taste.

Words/Expressions I hate on Dating Profiles
30/11/2015

LOL
Lady
Cheeky
Wicked sense of humour
Crap diem, sorry I mean Carpe Diem
Amusing
Normal
Laid back
Honest
Easy-going
Loving, sincere, loyal, caring, romantic
Sort of guy

I will love (suffocate) you
Friends would describe me as
My interests are
Football, golf, cycling, running, walking, train spotting, stamp collecting
My best friend is my dog
Apologies for
I find this so difficult
Introvert
Nice
Shy
Pleasant
Good company
All the normal things in life
I enjoy, cinema, theatre, eating out or quiet nights in
Equally at home in dress or wellies
Good conversation
Beach
Roaring log fire
Tattoo
Beard
Moustache
Bald
Turn-ons: skinny dipping
Dislikes: sarcasm
Looking for someone who's up for it

Exclamation marks

typo's

tbc

Lord give me strength. Why do I bother?

I think I might 'favourite' someone whose profile simply read:

"I am foul"

At last! A proposal of marriage after all these years!
06/01/2016

He just asked me to marry him!

So romantic and exciting!

This is how it happened...

A notification appeared on Googlemail saying that I had received an e-card.

I really, really hate e-cards, especially Christmas ones that arrive when you're at your busiest. They're just so cheapskate, unimaginative, naff and lazy. Birthday ones that prove the sender has forgotten all about you until the actual day are even worse. I'd much rather have nothing at all.

But a proposal of marriage is slightly different.

The copy goes:

Sexy Mary

Chocks away..Babe ! Are you still looking...Sensational..Stunning..Magnificent.. Gorgeous...Sensual..and Super Sexy... T S Eliot..xxx

and the animation is of a cuddly bear who dances around and finally goes down on one knee and says, "Will you Marry Me?"

It appears that you can get 'romantic' cards, 'kiss' cards, 'love' cards, 'cuddly cards and 'cute' cards, all from some online company called 123greetings.   Each one is accompanied by a very loud jolly tune, and costs the earth (and the sender) nothing.

My suitor first got in touch via a 'romantic' card, having seen me on 'Four

In A Bed'. I know nothing about him except that he lives in Nottingham and refers to himself as 'Flash Gordon'. We've never spoken, and actually, come to think of it, I don't even know what the bloke looks like! He's probably 5'4" with a beard and silly shoes.

So what. Wedding presents to Wydemeet please.

Fat Women
14/01/2016

Today I met a widower who only likes fat women.

I have been fantasizing about this chap for five years. He calls himself 'HotJames' and his profile is one of the most enchanting I have ever read. He so clearly misses his wife who has died, and describes how he would like to love again, how much he cares for his wonderful daughters, the garden with its statues, happy days spent at gymkhanas, and so on. The only part that I don't like is the bit at the end which says, "Sorry Mary of Devon, you're too thin" (still left in after five years, when I first contacted him, when I was only a size 12).

In the picture he looks totally yummy, grinning, with slightly too-long dark hair.

In his communications he is highly articulate.

He says he is unlikely to want to stay for lunch at the pub where we're planning to meet, because he has spent so much money over the years on no-hoper women.

We're meeting at the Wheatsheaf, a pub just outside Cricket St Thomas on my way to Mum's.

I pull up in the Golden Monster next to a jag which I think must be his.

And inside, there he is, looking nicely dressed, tall and distinguished.

So. Not a rebel at all. Nor is he bouncy, smiley or spontaneous. His mode of address is rather monotonic. He is very easy to chat to, but not so easy to bounce off. And it is bloody cold in this stupid restaurant area. I am beginning to feel like getting along on to Mum's.

He starts describing one of the 100s of people he has met who is a nurse who specialises in autism, and who apparently told him that he might be slightly Aspergers. He doesn't seem too upset by this, so I agree it might be true.

He explains that he wants a 'normal wife' who will move into his home and help him with his business etc. How are you going to find somebody at our age who is competent, who isn't already happy in a house of their own?" I query. "What's in it for them? Do you really just want a free housekeeper and business manager?"

I tell him that far from being a 'normal wife' I would like to change the world.

I've finished my shockingly expensive Spritzer (that he kindly paid for) and it's time to continue on (rather hungry by now I must confess) my journey to Mum's. It's been an interesting two hours.

But astonishing how different somebody can be in the flesh!

The Waldorf
14/01/2016

"Would you like to come with me to fire big guns in Las Vegas this Saturday?" asks Jock.

In the world of online dating you just never know who you're going to meet next, or what opportunities they are going to offer you.

Jock 'messaged' me during a train trip to London. By the time my train pulled in at Waterloo, we had discovered that he was taught by my father at Eton, and had arranged to meet at Covent Garden tube at 3.30pm.

One July, many moons ago, I organised The British Turkey Federation's Christmas Event with Michael Barry at the Waldorf, which is fairly close to the tube, so together we planned our assignation at their 'Palm Court' room for a tea dance.

He turned up in a scruffy denim jacket and a back-to-front baseball hat, only for us both to discover that Palm Court is now used for corporate conferences, and that afternoon tea in the restaurant starts at 12.30pm and ends at 4pm. *Ends*??

So we made do with some fig tea, sitting in a sort of passage, and quickly progressed on to Mumm rose champagne, la di dah.

Jock publishes a magazine about guns which has about 1000 subscribers including the army. He is also very involved in the divorce thing, and has self-published a book on the subject, just like me. Except that he has sold 400 copies of his book, compared with my mere 150.

We reminisced about so many mutual school friends, and then he and a mate of his, who had just turned up after consuming a several gallons of port at the Turf Club, accompanied me back to Embankment tube station, like true gents, where we all bid a fond farewell, and I headed back to jolly old Dartmoor.

What a shame I'm already busy this Saturday.

Vets
18/01/2016

I'd love to end up with a vet. I don't care if they're a bit poor relative to their intellect and working hours. I just think vets must be really nice.

So you can imagine how excited I was when my next online suitor told me that he was playing for a vets' rugby team that afternoon.

But when we finally got to speak he seemed a bit non-plussed. And then finally all became clear.

He meant veterans.

Six Women In A Kitchen
18/01/2016

Lindsey, Judith, Christabel, Diane, Abigail and I gather, vulture-like, around the hapless young Tesco man.

"My van's stuck in the drive outside in the snow," he stammers, depositing his Tesco green plastic crates in the middle of the floor, as we mentally count the number of Cava bottles included in this stash.

"Stay and join us for a drink!" shouts Lindsey, my Norwegian best mate, who has travelled from her home in Spain for this weekend.

"Would you like a blini?" enquires Christabel, over from her villa in Cyprus.

"Stay the night!" I order him. I'm fantasizing about a potential psychological thriller starring a Tesco man being trapped and terrorised by a group of six 50-something menopausal women.

This is 'the last hurrah' for Wydemeet. My bestest oldest mates from Exeter University have all come together here, from all over Europe, to say a final goodbye to my much-loved home, before it's sold - exchange is due in a couple of months' time.

We've been friends now for 38 years, and were last gathered together at Wydemeet on an equally chilly, snowy, New Years' Eve twenty years ago, just after Ex and I first bought the house, when wind whistled through window, door, floorboard and wall panel. And now here we are again, saying goodbye to the most luxurious and expensive B&B on Dartmoor.

This is the sort of party that the house is designed for. Every room is alive, bright, warm and welcoming. In front of the crackling log fire in the sitting room, we enjoy champagne that chilled in seconds in the snow outside the back door, using the only four glasses left that Judith gave us as a wedding present all that time ago; Neighbour's roast belted galloway is for dinner, which is already laid on the polished table in the candle-lit dining room; B&B left-overs comprise long brunches in the kitchen.

In the face of all this the Tesco man decides that perhaps he might be capable of reversing his truck backwards, downhill, in the ice, in the dark, and makes good his escape, never to be seen again.

The ladies, meanwhile, are back to their chat. We all believe we haven't changed at all since university days, oblivious to the wrinkles and saggy bits. Christabel is the best advert for HRT I have ever seen - she is radiant, exuding health and beauty, just as she did at university when she was followed around everywhere by a line of admirers. I have already asked her for a list of the vitamins, gels and sticky patches she uses, so that I can start looking like she does.

I have a selection of three dressing gowns of various thicknesses to wear during breakfast, as all of our personal inner thermostats are a bit wonky, and we get hot and flushed, or cold, rather more quickly these days than we used to do. Nobody comments if someone's face suddenly goes a bit red and/or sweaty. Not one of us seems keen to jump up and down on the trampoline anymore, and there's an urgent queue for the loo when we get back from our walks.

Another change is a sense of caution about getting lost, or skidding in our cars in the snow. There is quite a lot of talk about how to deal with our ageing parents, and our memories don't appear to be up to much anymore. But otherwise things are not all that different from nearly four decades ago.

Judith has grabbed my computer, She knows all my passwords and is busy examining this month's Top 20 single men on Encounters. She is really only interested in the Number One. He lives in Barnes and describes himself as a Winged Charioteer.

"That's from 'To His Coy Mistress' ", she says; and Abigail, quotes:

"Let us roll all our strength and all
Our sweetness up into one ball,
And tear our pleasures with rough strife
Through the iron gates of life.."

"... by Andrew Marvell," adds Christabel, who also read English at Exeter.

"Never heard of it, and now I must collect Faye from netball," I disappear out of the front door with Lindsey. "Just tell him, 'I am no coy mistress'" I shout back at them, as I depart.

On our return an hour later, the coven are beside themselves with excitement, as the Charioteer has replied by return,

"You're the only one that got it!!!"

The party who stayed behind has already devised a set of witty responses, as well as preparing the vegetables, but I suggest we just wait until he tries a little harder to impress me.

"Too many exclamation marks for someone who claims to be a writer anyway," snorts Abigail.

!!!!!??????????!!!!!!!!!!!

The Small World Of Online Dating
21/01/2016

"I hate him!" I cried.

Oh dear. I think I might have ballsed it up with Charioteer.

It turns out that some time ago I ran into his best mate, Charlie2110, on Encounters. I forwarded Charlie's profile to Judith, because I was busy at the time, they arranged to meet, and he stood her up! Upsetting her quite a lot! Unforgivable.

And now it turns out that Charioteer directed one of my most famous friends in a national TV sitcom in 2012; I am mates with his ex-girlfriend, and his ex-wife is mates with a great friend from school.

We speak the same too: "Call me old fashioned" and "cut of your jib" and "knock me down with a feather" all feature regularly in our parlance.

And we do the same things - like lying in bed tapping away on our computers all day, while other people work around us.

And I think I can provide what he wants:

"Vital, funny, clever, open, charismatic, sexy, curious, creative, energetic, talented, fit, adventurous, optimistic, irreverent, gregarious, warm, wild, empathetic and fun," are the list of attributes he requires in a partner.

"I can do all those falling off a log. In fact I might replace the words I've used to describe myself in my own profile with yours," I tell him. "Lucky you're not looking for anyone modest."

We spoke for an hour on the phone yesterday. We were chatting away happily and I finally managed to ask him to sit down and take a deep breath while I told him The Truth. That he'd been selected by committee, and that I'd never heard of Andrew Marvell, despite having studied Restoration Poetry for A'level.

New Potentials, Hurrah!
31/01/2016

"Exciting news, DelightfulMary! You have new Matches:

Artistic67
19 years ago i suffered renal failure and had to go on dialysis which lasted 12 years..

greensteve

I like all the usual things..

rancid09
I'm a tattooist..

PianomanPaul
My passion is my job; definitely a workaholic..."

The above, and I promise I haven't made anything up, is how this morning's crop of would-be lovers advertised themselves to the fairer sex in hope of life-long love and commitment.

Whether I'm subscribing or not, regular as clockwork every morning at 3.35am Encounters sends me details of six potential life-partners.

Winged Charioteer suggests that my next job should be writing profiles for such people.

"But when they actually meet someone they'll be really boring in real life!" I wailed.

Nevertheless, after 30 minutes of lengths in a very crowded health club pool, I'm beginning to think that his idea might have legs. Watch this space!

I am so Excited!!
04/02/2016

"I am lovable! Love me!"

Well that's what we want to write, but we can't, can we?

So what do we put instead, to maximise our chances of being noticed by our potential life soulmate?

Stuck?

I am here to help you get noticed by somebody who could change your life for the better, forever.

This is the start of my new website, and my new life! All thanks to Winged Charioteer's inspired suggestion! I could kiss him - if I ever actually met him!

I'm going to help people write better internet dating profiles. I've called myself www.profile-writer.com, and I'm pleased with what I've done so far.

I shall be doing the one thing that, as an erstwhile PR professional, I am really properly trained for and experienced at. A job that I had thought was dead, defunct and obsolete. In effect, I will be writing endless press releases for these people, of 250 words each. That's what I really love doing. But instead of being about dehydrated casserole sauce mix, disposable lavatory seat covers, polar explorers etc, now my press releases are going to be all about love!

And what's more, I can write them from absolutely anywhere, so I no longer need to feel chained to remotest Devon. I can run this business from London, Australia - even from a luxury yacht in the Caribbean! I am footloose and fancy free and can be with anyone, anywhere, whilst my work will be enjoyable, constructive and lucrative.

How brilliant is that?!

Even if my customers do turn out to be utterly turgid in real life, having blagged a meeting with some stunna, via my inimitable prose - that's their problem, not mine.

I am also poised on the edge of my seat, hoping that the conveyancers might start tomorrow on the paperwork so that I can buy the perfect house for the children, the horses, Twiglet and me, which I've found not far from Exeter. And, again thanks to Winged Charioteer, I've managed to blag £5,000 off its owners' 'rock bottom price'. He told me to haggle because of its lack of central heating, even though I would have paid their asking price anyway.

Liver Cirrhosis
05/02/2016

"With all due respect, I'm not sure that you will attract members of the fairer sex by telling them you've suffered from cirrhosis of the liver," I write to Napoleon1815, a 69 year old ex-international banker from Dorchester, who turned up on my Encounters 'Perfect Matches' at 3.30am today. "Would you like me to help you re-write your profile for free, as one of my first three guinea pigs?"

This is the brainwave I've just had, as to how to market my new service. Clever eh? I suspect my commercial message will get censored by interfering nosy Big Brother at Encounters' headquarters, but it's worth a punt. I'll let you know what happens!

10 Worst Profiles
08/02/2016

I've lost confidence that countless lonely hearts will proactively google my new profile writing service.

Napoleon came back to me saying he felt he had to be honest about his liver condition, that despite including news of it in his profile he'd already been messaged eight times, and would I like to chat?

I emailed back saying eight young Russian prostitutes hoping to marry him in the expectation that he'll soon drop down dead don't count.

I see that he has now taken my advice and there's nothing about his stupid liver on Encounters anymore, but of course I didn't get paid for helping him, did I?

So I've had another idea.

I shall 'message' people with truly awful profiles who've been hanging around on Encounters for ages, offering my assistance.

So I've put 'lady', 'cosy', 'cuddles', 'football','gsoh' and even 'ill' into Encounters' 'keywords search', but nothing's come up.

I tried again, with 'private school' and 'ha ha' to see what happened. Nothing.

YAH
24/02/2016

A bloke calling himself YAH just messaged me. He doesn't look like a yah in the least. His pics show him with dyed dark brown hair, tinted glasses, a black shirt, a classic E-type, small aeroplane and infinity pool. And he comes from Torquay. So I replied with "some people call me a yah".

If he were a proper yah he would be displaying a dead pheasant in his profile picture, and wearing Le Chameau wellies.

Well he's just responded informing me that YAH means Young At Heart.

Fine Day
24/02/2016

"Yes, the geography isn't favourable. As a mere autodidact myself I was intrigued by your 'understands private education' observation? I am, you must appreciate, a neophyte at this business and somewhat pusillanimous about the entire procedure."

This was FineDay's response to my approach which went: "It's a bugger you live half-way across the world."

As far as I can make out, he's some literary name-dropping impoverished slightly pompous Marc Bolan look-alike marina owner, with an extraordinary vocabulary, expelled from a secondary modern when he was 14 ½ years old.

Norfolk Man of Mystery
02/03/2016

I sent FineDay a short vid of me playing The Moonlight Sonata, looking mournful and lonely.

"...your playing drew me into the room and for a moment I understood why I have spent my life, till now, swerving to avoid good fortune...I'm really afraid you could make me happy," he emailed me back.

"All the love I have left in this world
I have rolled into a small ball
Lodged like a sweet wrapper
In the corner of my jacket pocket.

Every so often, unconsciously,
I put my hand in my pocket
And turn the tiny package
Between my thumb and index finger,

Like a blackbird turning its egg.

Whilst you were playing, did you feel my finger caress your cheek as I gently flicked your hair behind your ear?"

I'm in love. Fantasizing about the 'what if' with this highly talented, sensitive, very funny and flattering man. Yet I don't know what he looks like. I don't even know his proper name. And I haven't heard back from him again.

Ugh. I hate this internet dating bollocks. It really messes with your head.

Dearth of Single Men
02/03/2016

There's a splutter at the end of the phone line.

Then Helen manages to speak intelligibly through her giggles. "This man just came in to have lunch with his sister," she croaks (Helen is on reception at my mate's Prince Hall Hotel down the road).

"They saw your book for sale on reception and the sister said, 'She looks nice.'

" 'She is nice' I said, and anyway, the long and the short of it is that we've got his email address (he owns a five-bedroomed house in Yealmpton) and we've taken a picture. Would you like us to send them to you?"

"Well yes please, obviously," I reply.

So 'ping', here they are on my email, and I have a sudden thought.

"Is this the bloke you've set me up with for Thursday?" (I have forwarded his details on to Karen, who has arranged a double-blind-date for us both later in the week.)

So yes. That's exactly who it is. I was right. It would appear that currently there are just two middle-aged single blokes available in the whole of South Devon.

You Can't Be Too Careful
02/03/2016

In the middle of the pitch black night I descend down a wild, narrow lane into what looks like a sort of private carpark, in my filthy Gold Monstrosity truck, and by the wavering light of my old torch, stumble the 400 yards, all alone as ever, to the large front door of the stately home.

I push it ajar, and inside is a sea of anonymous black ties and late-middle-aged ladies in long dresses. I don't recognise a soul here. They're all missing their riding hats.

It's the local hunt annual dinner, and I find myself seated at the end of a trestle table with nobody opposite me, nor anyone to one side.

"Why oh why did I come?" flits through my mind as I tuck into my smoked salmon and prawns.

But, oh gosh! The Chairman of the Hunt comes over and deposits himself in the empty chair next to me, meanwhile I am very much included in the juicy conversation of the rest of the table. Things are beginning to pick up, as a beautiful chicken breast stuffed with spinach and swilling in cream arrives.

Across the table, one of the most stunning young women I have ever seen declares that she met her partner through Muddy Matches.

"Oh - I'm on Encounters," I regale the table.

"Have you met Michael Whiteley-Sprocket?" queries the very pretty and jolly young woman one away from me. She has a sweet little pony tail.

"Been there, done that, like everyone else in the South West," I reply. "Bit odd and slightly camp. Why, have you too?"

"Yes, he's my ex-husband," she says.

Four Johns
03/03/2016

I've still got four Johns, as well as a Richard on the go at the moment, and my double-date with hotel man and his mate Don tonight.

If anything comes out of any of it, I will consume my hat, with some relish.

Stranded
04/03/2016

"Why's my breathalyser bleeping like that?" I said. "Is 0.1 more than 0.08? Oh my god, I'm over the limit!"

It was midnight in Totnes carpark, and I had been demonstrating my special gadget to Don, after a very slow and what would appear to have been rather insubstantial Italian dinner, judging by how little I'd had to drink compared with sometimes, and the clear impact of the alcohol on my system.

So I couldn't get in my car, but instead had to make my way back to Karen's house for a couple of coffees, rather embarrassingly putting the kibosh on any ulterior plans Don might have been harbouring regarding our kind hostess.

I blew into my breathalyser again, but it still measured 0.09, whereas 0.08 is the legal limit, so I was stranded, and went up to Karen's spare bedroom, registering that I seemed to be seeing two of everything, where there had previously been one earlier on in the evening.

I woke at 4.30am, dragged myself back up to the carpark and home, where, in the glare of my headlights, there appeared to be a herd of Dartmoor ponies wandering around my garden. They had to be rounded up and got rid of immediately, no matter what. So I did that, went back to bed, only to discover that this morning my thigh-length black suede boots are covered in mud.

'The boys', Derek and Don, our double blind dates, are both MAMILs with thin legs and jolly smiles.

"You look strong," Don had observed to me at one point in the evening. It turns out that I have met Don before - he plays squash with Michael W-S, the ex-husband I have just mentioned.

"I'm a swimmer. And come from a rowing family - it's in the genes," I retorted. But I have to accept that if I flung myself into either of these boys' arms with enthusiastic abandon, they would both fall over.

5 More Of The Same

Rugby Playing Poet
12/03/2016

"Oh God! I kissed him once! He had long curly blond hair, pink tinted glasses, a purple open top sports car, tight jeans and cowboy boots!" I exclaimed.

We're talking about the legendary Tom Briscoe, the coolest poser in the second year at Exeter back in 1978, who, it turns out, is the best friend of Roland - today's lunchtime blind date, from Northamptonshire. Tom, I gather, is (predictably) now divorced, and living on the Isle of Wight.

Roland is combining meeting me with a visit to old friends who live in Yelverton. We have an interest in food retail business in common. He's also into motor-racing and flying, and describes himself as 5'11" and 'stocky'. His daughter went to Cambridge, so he and/or his ex-wife must be brainy, and he got expelled from both Oundle and Bedford schools. I am looking forward to finding out what for.

Meanwhile Winged Charioteer, who had been purloined by some more local 'gorgeous girl', appears to be back on the market, and is due in for a very serious op to be conducted by robots this Tuesday. He is so highly articulate, I am loving communicating with him. He writes things like "what is the real-politic of Life if not a series of deals, pacts, barters, quid-pro-quos, understandings and entente-cordials???" God knows, so I wrote back that entente cordials sound quite nice, but I prefer elderflower. I really deeply hope I get to meet him in the end.

And now, most exciting of all, a great bear of a man calling himself Sir James, has sent me two long and beautifully written poems, and a video of himself singing "You were always on my mind" in a band of over 60s in a Devon village hall. His voice on the answerphone is just lovely - even posher than mine - and his humour is gentle and funny. I have implored him not to waste himself on father-figure-searching/gold-digging skinny little 25 year old dolly birds hoping for him to die. And I've sent him my sad, lonely, and bereft-looking video selfie - velfie? seleo? - of me playing the Moonlight Sonata, wearing a coat.

Sir James lives in a 10 bedroom house in Sussex, but knows my little corner of Devon well. He has left millions of midnight emails, and today he's attending the farmers' lunch at his local point to point, having delivered two Aberdeen Angus calves in the early hours. He sounds as excited by all of this as I am! Watch this space for yet another near-miss failure!!

Giant of a Man
15/03/2016

We've spoken at last.

He's bigger in stature, confidence and personality than I am.

He sounds like Elvis, and looks like a craggy grandpa man-mountain.

He comes from the same world (the posher end) as mine, and does horses, music, and writes. Who else combines all those things, apart from me?

So now I've got butterflies. Haven't felt those for ages - months, years!

Where (if anywhere) is this all going to lead?

He hung up, saying he was off to the pub round the corner for pint. That we'd go out for a meal when he's down next week, looking at Devon-based farms for his son, when we would chat again.

I can't wait that long!!!!!!!!!!!!!!!!!!!!!!!

Ideal Match
25/03/2016

"I'm cheerful, easy-going, warm, kind, empathetic, decent, and loyal.

Confident, charismatic, sorted, solvent, sexy, and posh.

Modest and humble.

My favourite thing is bringing a smile to the faces of those around me.

I live in a large house in remotest Dartmoor, but am very mobile and time rich, so more than happy to come and see you.

I make a sort of living from chatting, and occasionally cleaning lavatories."

My ideal match:

Oh no! Are you sitting comfortably?

My ultimate dream man would combine sensuality with a really good sense of humour (not necessarily at the same time, nor in that order).

He would be big, both in stature and presence; provocative, original, thoughtful and articulate.

'Bien dans sa peau', he would be on top of his game, his own man, straightforward and free of hang-ups/issues; kind, and emotionally intelligent.

He would be at home in a largely privately educated crowd.

Young(ish) in both body and spirit, hair on head as opposed to face, he would typically be wearing a broad grin.

He'd be cultured and sporty; urban and rural.

He would be looking for a stimulating, loving, committed relationship.

And he could make me do the nose trick.

Dream on, Mary!"

Well the above has taken me hours and hours and hours to craft. So many hours, in truth, that anyone would think I was obsessed.

And, discovering that I have actually described my idealised Rugby-Playing Poet as my perfect partner above, looking at it again I think I have also described myself. So perhaps such a man ought really to exist, and not be just a dream?

Anyway, so what's happened as a result?

"it looks to me as though you could well be on the free loaders list that should be avoided - load of bullshit. I will by-pass you and go on to see my mates."

Oh dear. That was Roland. We had a perfectly enjoyable lunch together (that he paid for), but I felt he wouldn't be strong enough to stand up to me, so told him about RPP. Ooops.

Anyway, 24hrs later, and, amongst a sudden surge of suitors, someone from Dublin going by the name of 'Unsure_About_This' writes: *"Your profile is up there with the Magna Carta and Ulysses, a work of art. Are you related to Spike Milligan?"*

So I'm feeling dead chuffed that it seems to have worked, and I'm not planning on fiddling around with it any further.

I have the best crop ever of online dates at the moment.

RRP has come in from the cold and last night we had an hour's chat at 12.30am, inbetween his 200 cows calving. I love his posh gentle caressing voice. I suggested he whisked Faye and me away for Sunday lunch on our return to Gatwick after next week's skiing holiday. I wonder whether that will happen.

A chap calling himself Mr B has two homes, was an investment banker for twenty years, and has been selling gin palaces for ten. Encounters Big Brother says we are a 98% match for each other.

"Guess how many boats I have sold and what my ex-wife is called?" he challenged me. *"320 and Mary. Would you like to meet up in Bath?"*

Well I'm a bit busy with the children home for the Easter holidays right now, but I can't wait to speak to him later today.

I also have a 67 year old ex-racing driver on the go, and Winged Charioteer is back in touch, after his prostate operation.

So what is going to happen to me next?

"The pen is SO powerful!" I breathed to RPP, as we reluctantly hung up at 1.45am.

But none of these gorgeous men has seen me for real, let alone in a swimming costume, or less.

Yesterday afternoon, Marks & Spencer's changing room mirror revealed what a truly hideous sight I have become.

Brief Encounter
07/04/2016

South West Trains has an offer on, which means you can travel anywhere in their network for only £15, if you buy a day return ticket. Or £5 if you're under 16.

This skiing holiday costs just £399 (including flight, transfers, accommodation and all you can eat) each for Faye and me - almost as cheap as staying at home! The trouble is the flight leaves Gatwick for Andorra at 5.25am.

Well I have a cunning plan.

We subtly park the Gold Monstrosity in a residential street of Pinhoe, on the outskirts of Exeter. We walk up the high street, pulling our enormous rattling suitcases behind us (thank God it's not raining), stand on the titchy unsheltered platform, and catch a rattly old slow train to Clapham Junction.

Here we are met by Adrian - an online date who has arranged all of this for us, who lives ten minutes' walk from the station. He buys us a Costa's, we have a quick chat, and then it's on to Gatwick.

We walk 50 yards from Gatwick's railway station in the Southern Terminal, around the back of WH Smith, to the 'Yotel', and for £48 spend the rest of the evening shacked up in bed in our little pods, watching telly, tucking into delicious prawns and smoked salmon at 3 for £10 which we've bought from M&S, just opposite Smiths.

At 4am we emerge, not exactly refreshed, but excited at least, to check in for our flight at a desk located just beyond M&S.

Couldn't be easier! Isn't modern life great?

I text a thank you to Adrian. He is one of the most eligible men I have met through Encounters. Educated, presentable, polite and organised. He is an auctioneer for collectibles - mostly those mugs with pictures of the various King Georges on them.

Well he's really nice, but for once there's a lot of competition at the moment.

I wonder whether nothing will come of something - the normal pattern?

Demelza and Ross
07/04/2016

She's called Demelza.

Her partner is called Ross.

This Demelza is a real live person.

She used to live in the tree adjacent to Swampy's, until she was five months pregnant and had to climb down.

She was a traveller and she boasts numerous piercings.

Ross had to go to prison for a year, for the part he played in 1999's 'Carnival Against Capitalism' riots outside the House of Commons.

"Fancy that?!" I said, as I handed round the greens. "I took part in the Countryside Alliance march a couple of years later!"

These days Demelza lives with her two sons in a cob cottage, just a stone's throw from where I'm planning to live, a few miles outside Exeter.

But for the moment we are sharing a locker for our skis, on a mountainside somewhere in the Pyrenees.

I'm A Real Live Daily Mail Victim!
08/04/2016

He's a con man!

And I'm the victim! Like all those other idiotic plain fat middle-aged women you read about in the Daily Mail who give away all their money to

Nigerians, Moroccans and Greek waiters.

I've just returned from a dinner with my iconic superstar film star friend (who now lives in the middle of nowhere in Spain, down the road from Lindsey, having once resided in the shack at the end of my lane in Dartmoor) who by pure chance now happens to be making a visit to Andorra coinciding with mine.

Feeling curious, I started digging around on Google to see if I could find out something about my singing rugby player's surname/baronetcy title.

Sitting in Faye's and my en-suite bathroom so as not to disturb her sleeping self, perched on the lavatory, with my laptop propped up on the bidet in front of me, and my vape beside me on the floor, I am breaking out into a cold sweat.

Here is the truth:

RPP is not 61 - he's 71. He's not a baronet. And he's gone bust to the tune of £2.5m. And he's got a wife called Susan and three grown up sons, and there's no sign of any legal qualification, even though he said he was a lawyer.

With some apprehension, I email him saying that my computer is insisting that he's 71, not 61, and am I going bonkers?

He emails me back, assuring me that he is "a hale and hearty 61, born in 1954."

So I've done some more digging around, and guess what.

Companies House confirms everything I feared.

There's a vid on YouTube that is most definitely him playing the guitar and singing in a hotel in Crete.

He has been the subject of a BBC South investigative programme.

AND the subject of a long Ofcom report, resulting from another 'Rogue Trader' programme about him screened in 2012 on Channel 5. His complaints of unfair representation were dismissed.

Perhaps the service should be renamed Of Con.

His actions appear to have left around 30 elderly couples homeless, while he has put his ten bedroom farmhouse in Sussex in his son's name and still lives there, and the report says he continues to drive around in a new Range Rover with personalised number plates.

I am chastened, saddened, mortified, and rather frightened. My first potentially really bad experience through online dating. The sort of thing everybody warns you about. So this is what it feels like.

Yet all I have lost, compared with so many the other poor sucker middle aged women, is hope.

Con Man?
10/04/2016

I thought that, with his cover blown, Mr Con Man would simply disappear from the ether.

But no! He's straight back, more charming than ever! I am seduced and confused! I can't think straight while attempting to remain upright on a pair of skis. Am I being unfair? Should one judge a person simply from what's written about them, without giving them the opportunity to speak out?

He assures me in words of one syllable of his full name, title, and his 'hale and hearty' age.

How do you argue, short of saying 'prove it' - which only proves that any trust left in the relationship has entirely disappeared.

So I give in, and contact our mutual Devon-based friend, to find out what she knows about him.

"Don't touch him with a barge pole!" she shoots back by email. "Don't do anything until we've spoken! Have you read about him on the internet?!"

Brief Encounter 2
10/04/2016

We rose at 2.30am, in time to throw on some clothes, grab breakfast, and catch the coach from the ski resort to some obscure titchy airport in Spain, from which we were eventually flown back to Gatwick.

Round the corner from Arrivals to the train station, and 45 minutes later we're back in the cafe on Clapham Junction Station's Platform 14, sipping capuccinos, this time with Ex (who lives down the road) who has brought his girlfriend's daughter, and our son Will along with him, to snatch a precious ten minutes between trains with darling Faye.

And all too soon, it's back to Pinhoe; stopping at every pretty little station along the way, almost all of which hold some happy memory for Faye and me.

We declined to meet Granny and Twiglet at Crewkerne, because that would have meant yet another 'Brief' Encounter of two hours in the very pleasant cafe there, which we felt was just too long, after such an endless journey.

So we'll meet them tomorrow at the 'New Health Club' in Exeter, instead.

The Gold Monstrosity is still sitting happily in the rain in Pinhoe High Street. Someone has folded in the front mirror, but otherwise all is OK.

So after a 16hr journey, Faye and I finally arrive home, to discover that the boiler, which was mended two days before setting out, has stopped working again, and the house is like a fridge.

The Baronet Who Probably Isn't
12/04/2016

I've had a brainwave.

I don't think it's fair to write off somebody just because of what is written on the internet about them.

So I am going to call his bluff.

I am going to offer to write an article in the Daily Mail for my Rugby Playing Poet. It's going to be one of those stories about fat middle-aged women who get ripped off by Greek waiters exploiting their loneliness and vulnerability.

The difference is going to be that my little feature is going to end with a twist. It's going to be called 'The Baronet Who Is' and will prove that I haven't been led up the garden path after all, and my man really is telling the truth, and has been shamelessly maligned by the internet.

The catch is, that RPP is going to have to come up with back-up evidence for everything he has told me, in order for me to be able to run the story successfully.

We will both benefit. Anytime he is googled, there will be a Daily Mail story refuting all the bad stuff on him on the internet.

Meanwhile, I will also benefit from some free PR, as the feature will end with the words: "You can find Mary Hadow's first book, 'Dare B&B' on Amazon, priced £5.99."

So I email him with my brilliant suggestion. He will need to confirm his age, his baronetcy and his legal qualifications; and his ex-wife will need to contribute a few enthusiastic words too; so that the final picture in the Daily Mail is of him and me, and possibly his wife and family too, all smiling together because he's such a jolly good bloke who has been so unfairly misrepresented.

He emails back, in tears, at my 'blind faith' in him, after all the terrible untruths and abuse that have so unfairly been hurled at him over the past decade.

I assure him that this is an exercise to benefit both of us, and it is imperative that he is utterly truthful with me if I am going to be able to progress with my plan. We speak - as usual at nearly midnight, and, as usual, his mobile signal keeps petering out, 'but there's no landline in the house' - he'll have to go out to the office and use the landline there.

His age - he'll send me lots of pictures to show how young-looking he is. His title - it's complicated, he'll tell me when we meet. His living arrangements and relationship with his wife - it's complicated....

In the morning, after this roller coaster month of communications with him, I send him a 'Dear James' email, saying that I'm so sorry, but I simply don't trust him enough to go ahead with my proposed project. I press 'send' and take the horses out for a trot in the April sunshine.

I come back to a long, sad, and understanding email from him, quietly accepting that I won't take any further calls from him.

I listen to his answerphone message.

"Hello," he says. "I would like to book an entire team of 22 rugby players into your B&B next month if you have the availability please?"

Oh he is so very funny and charming. But he's 71. I'm sure of it. That's too old for me. And anyway. Much worse. He lied about it. Twice now. I think.

What Are Things Coming To?
22/04/2016

Am I going completely mad?

I woke in the early hours this morning feeling suddenly very clear-headed.

I have been mooning around fantasizing about a 71 yr old man who economises with the truth, whose company is in administration, and who lives on the other side of the country, just because he is funny, charming, musical, whimsical, comes from the same background and is bigger than me.

This is nonsense! I have been on my own for too long!

More visits to the Exeter Golf and Country Club required - the only place I know of where you can always be sure to find a gaggle/swarm/herd/flotilla/caddyful of single, male Over-50s. I must learn to like zig-zag jumpers.

Fourth In A Bed
22/04/2016

"I studied Philosophy, Psychology, Mathematics and Physics - so am well versed with Schroedinger's cat (my great claim to fame is my great uncle is Bertrand Russell)," writes Boris, who, having just watched the fourth re-run of Channel 4's Show in which I came last, made up the 'Fourth In A Bed' sobriquet.

He is my new Numero Uno correspondent at the moment. He was one of several who rang and wrote to me, in a bid to reassure me that it was 'them, not me' which meant Wydemeet did so badly in the reality TV B&B competition.

I have sold one more book, one more kindle, and received one more B&B booking as a result of today's repeat of the programme, and 550 views of my website.

Boris tells me that he would have liked to have been a concert jazz pianist but his fingers aren't long enough. I wonder if it's true, what they say about small hands, small wotsit. He has also been a Canadian logger, and once woke to find a bear in his tent.

Anyway - clearly it's not only Blackpool housewives who watch the programme, and hopefully Boris will buy my book, and come for a visit before Wydemeet is sold. He sounds like a most interesting person.

I expect he is short and bearded, like most of them.

This Just Feels Weird
10/05/2016

"Have you read all that stuff about him on the internet?" enquires one-eyed Simon, as he joins we two Moorland Women of Substance - Lydia, who is acrimoniously divorced and has been left with a massive pile which she rents out on top of Exmoor, and me - at our large empty table.

Lydia and I have repaired to her local pub for supper. There is nowhere to cook the packet macaroni cheese she's bought for us, at her freezing cold house. Nowhere to sit, and nothing to eat it with, or off.

"... and how come you met him through online dating?"

I bite back my retort that online dating is quite a normal place to come across online dates.

"His lovely wife, Sue, would sit at that table with one or both of their sons, while he wandered around the pub chatting to everybody and singing songs," continues Simon. "We miss him. He was a great character and really cheered everyone up."

Everything around me is beginning to feel a bit murky, out of focus, as if it's swaying and surreal, and I don't think this is a result of our bottle of Pinot Grigio (the only wine this pub stocks). It turns out that last year RPP had rented a house for his family just a couple of miles away from here. That he spent a considerable amount of time helping Lydia going through her finances; and that his family entertained her to dinner at their rental home once or twice. Her house, the pub, the moor - all around there's a sense of darkness - menacing loneliness, uncertainty, despair lying not far below our jolly banter.

But maybe this is how remotest Exmoor always feels. It's certainly quite a lot different from, say, Parson's Green.

Does He Really Exist?
11/05/2016

"I bet he'll ring to say his car's broken down and he can't come," I think to myself, as I hastily apply Boots No 7 Beautifully Matte Mousse Light As Air For A Flawless Finish to my pink damp face, sweaty from the jacuzzi and the boiling hot ladies' changing room of my new club.

Two days ago RPP emailed to say that he would be looking at houses near Launceston on Monday, and should we meet up. I replied that I was already booked to meet Kate, an old university friend, for lunch, and my Thunderbirds group of female friends for dinner, but that I could work something out, around all of that. Not expecting for a minute that my mystery man actually exists, let alone will show.

I've arranged to meet him for lunch at the club at 12.30pm, swiftly followed by a second lunch with Kate at 1.30pm.

As I wait outside in the club garden, trying to cool down, my mobile rings. It's him.

"My car's broken down," he says.

No surprises there, then.

"So I won't be with you til 1pm - is that alright?"

Well blow me down, he really is on his way! I still don't quite believe it.

But I wander into the restaurant anyway, to reserve a table, and my, my - here he is! He absolutely doesn't look 71 - he's tall, about 6'1"; slightly overweight (which I quite like); white haired and bearded (which he has warned me about); and is smiling and laughing and full of fun and warmth, handing me an envelope which turns out to have £35 in it.

"Instead of flowers - you said you preferred cash," he reminds me.

As he courteously takes charge, he makes me feel giggly and flirty, and I realise that I'm smiling a lot. Kate arrives shortly after. Kate is still happily married to the man she met at Exeter University 38 years ago. She's lived in the same house in Wimbledon for over 25 years, she works locally in market research, and has three grown-up responsible sons. She vicariously enjoys my relatively wild, exciting life, and pretends to be shocked by the current scenario. The three of us make an unlikely, but merry trio in the as-always-empty grand restaurant.

After rather a lot of Marlborough Valley Sauvignon, still grinning, I get in my truck, and my date and I race up the A30 in convoy to view the first of his houses. We're 30 minutes late. The estate agent is not amused. And assumes that I am Mrs RPP.

I am now running late, miles from my dinner-venue, so rather rudely I dump "Sir James" somewhere in mid-Devon, and fly off, leaving him to work out where he is, and what he's going to do next.

The following morning, still in bed as usual at about 11am, I am immersed in a long row on the phone with the hideous Booking.com, when I hear voices below my window.

It's HIM!!!

I rush down with my unenhanced 'first thing' look - yesterday's make-up, morning-breath, dull, tangled hair .... lucky I'm in my Four In A Bed sleeping attire, including my nylon-looks-a-bit-like-silk dressing gown, over crumpled floral pyjamas.

It's a bit embarrassing to be looking like this, sitting across the table from a married man, but anyhow, I make us some proper coffee, chat for a bit; and then I have to leave for Faye's riding lesson, while he drives home to his wife and family in Sussex. Via Spooky One-Eyed Simon's pub on top of The Other Moor.

Adonis
17/05/2016

"Ah - that'll be Jim," says Bob, one my favourite men, Elsie's husband, whom I've known since pre-NCT days - for 17 years in fact.

I've just explained to Bob that my next blind date is a good-looking chap who has recently joined Dartmouth Yachtclub.

"He's really, really nice," Bob continues.

So, more optimistic than usual, I bowl into the pub for my Encounter, and skid to a halt in amazement. There, straight in front of me, is the best-looking 60-something man I have ever seen. Knocks George Clooney into a cocked hat.

He gives me the kindest, warmest smile which reaches right to his eyes. He's all chiselled features, and beautifully dressed slim height. He's leaning against the bar waiting for me, he has recognised me immediately, and he stands up to kiss me hello.

"You two known each other for a long time then?" observes the drunk, who has been standing next to my Adonis, at the bar.

"We've been married for 35 years and we've got two children," I reply, all smiles.

I'm a bit annoyed that I haven't worn heels which make me look thinner, as this chap's tall enough for that to have been OK.

We chat outside, order our food, sit down at our table. I am my normal amazingly engaging entertaining self. Never failed yet in 50+ encounters.

"I'm looking for a soul mate with whom I would want to spend all my time,

24/7," he says.

"Agh, bollocks to that," I remark. "At our age we need a break, get a bit of our own space. I'd go for more like four days a week or something, keeping our own houses. Urrrr.. Ummmm... sounds wonderful, um in principle, idealistic, errrr," and collapse into silence, realising I've made a bit of a goof.

Jim, it turns out, is new to Encounters, and has already received 350 messages. He has planned a trip up to Birmingham, taking in several beauties on the way, including my mate Judith's glamorous neighbour in Cheltenham - my New Forest date's old flame. Their date is due to take place in just a couple of days' time.

Jim looks at his watch without even pretending not to. It's only 10.15pm and he hasn't even ordered coffee, let alone pudding. Suddenly he clearly can't wait to get away from me.

I get back home alone and reach for my vape.

I am indignant.

"He'll be back in a year, when he's discovered that his other 350 fans are all lying, bitter, neurotic, needy, unbalanced alcoholics," I comfort myself.

The Titchy World That Is Online Dating
19/05/2016

Treehugger, one of my favourite online date platonic mates, is taking part in the '75km Dartmoor Cycle Race' this weekend, and has come to stay for a couple of nights.

It is nearly midnight, and here we are, sitting comfortably side by side at the kitchen table, our computers propped up in front of us, taking a cheeky peak at what each others' 'fans' look like on the Encounters website that we both subscribe to.

"That's James Hutton!" exclaims Treehugger, as we look at the picture of my recent Clapham Junction Brief Encounter. "I know him really well! I'm having dinner with him tomorrow!"

I gaze at the page of very beautiful girls who are Treehuggers' many fans.

Suddenly I burst out: "That's Jill! The one who lives opposite my great friend in Cheltenham, who is meeting Adonis this weekend, and keeps that bloke I met in the New Forest hotel as a sort of pet!" I exclaim.

"I took her out for lunch last weekend - too rich for me," responds Treehugger. "And she told me that she was new to all this!!"

Volvo or Maserati?
13/08/2016

It's been four years.

I am finally going to meet up with Mr NoButYesButNo. A 6'2" intellectual grinning hunk of manhood, Number 1 in the Encounters Most Popular Hit Parade, who has patiently and politely courted me throughout this time while I remained under the impression that his messages came from mad weirdo boring orange haired Peter from South Africa. I can't believe I have managed to waste all this time, and that NoButYesButNo has stayed with me, despite endless rude retorts from me to his courteous messages, me mistakenly believing he was that troll Peter, despite the huge amount of temptation he has inevitably been subjected to from his many Encounters fans.

My ailing Gold Monstrosity has managed the 50 miles to drop Faye off at her sleepover, despite a few splutters, and I stagger into the carpark of the pub NBYBN, who has driven down from Bristol, has kindly and intelligently booked for our supper.

There are only two cars in the carpark. On the left is an old red Volvo, dulled with age; and on the right is a pristine sparkly new black Maserati. I park between them and stride into the empty pub, trembling with curiosity and apprehension.

"So which is it - the Volvo or the Maserati?" I challenge the large, smiley rugby-player-type bloke as he stands to greet me.

"You guess. Which do you think it is?"

Bingo! The Maserati! Yeay!!! This is all just too, too perfect!

A rich clever unaffected slightly overweight gent! Hurrah! At last! And I am fascinated. He is a recently retired Vice Chancellor of a Poly-turned-University, and these guys earn significantly more than the Prime Minister! Quite rightly, in a sort of a way, I suppose. As really they are running these academic establishments as quite large profit-generating businesses, with a vast staff and assets, just like any company's managing director. Proper businessmen earning proper businessmen's salaries. Driving Maseratis.

And then guess what. We get to discussing our online experiences and hey-ho, no surprises - his last date was with Jill of Cheltenham, and there she is on his 'recents' site, in full, beautiful, thin glory. It would appear that she and I have now dated at least four of the same men!!

So. The big question. Is it love? He has everything!

Alas! He says 'cheers'. Call me a small-minded, intolerant, old-fashioned bigot, but I can't be doing with that.

Flowers vs Cheque
15/08/2016

"You maaake me feeeeel, miiiightee reeeal!" I am singing along to Ken Bruce's show on Radio 2 at the top of my voice, meanwhile achieving my B&B hospital corners in great style.

My spirits are ridiculously high today. The B&B is ticking along in its jolly well-oiled efficient and profitable fashion, with a delightful Swiss family staying, who are enjoying the walks that I am suggesting for them, and who aren't interested in putting me to the trouble and expense of cooked breakfasts.

But most of all - my online date, Stephen, with whom I've been communicating for about six weeks now - is coming to visit me tomorrow, on his way home to Staffordshire from a five-day break in St Ives.

In his profile he says he will have me 'in stitches'. Speaking to him a couple of times on the phone, he sounds quite dour Brummie and he isn't smiling in his online pics (one is of him in a horses' tackshop which is what drew me to him in the first place). His emails are gradually becoming more light-hearted and funnier though, and he has just been head-hunted by Australia to sort out their IT security problems. 'Name your price!' they said, having interviewed him twice over the phone at midnight during the weekend. So that's pretty impressive. He must be a lot brainier than I am.

Also he turns out to be a bit of a mix between computer IT nerd, and Pisces. Interesting. To me at any rate.

While he loves DIY, and is obviously very adept at computers, his favourite piece of music is Clair de Lune, which I can play a bit, and he called me 'darling' the other day. Perhaps he had imbibed a little too much of the golden nectar. He's only 48, so in comparison I am a wrinkly old bag.

He has already stood me up twice: both times blaming the distance/traffic challenges. Then he could have come to see me on his way to St Ives, rather than on his way home, or I could have visited him there - none of which has transpired, and none of which have concerned me overly, because there has been too much other stuff going on for me to give him my full attention.

So now it's about to happen. We're going to meet at last! I put out some clean clothes, set the alarm so I can have a bath before preparing breakfast, and try to sleep despite my excitement. He is due at 10am, just as my Swiss family finishes their continental breakfast.

I whizz down early in the morning to the kitchen, all of a fluster - how will I remember the breakfast orders when all I can think of is meeting this man? I have suggested that we walk together today to Prince Hall Hotel for lunch - what could be more magical?

I casually check my laptop as I move to put the kettle on the AGA. "Sorry Mary - I can't come. There's no point. We live too far apart from each other," he wrote at 7.30 this morning.

"Well it would have been kinder, braver, and more sensible to have said that to me in person," I bark back in a very upset email, and spill the coffee.

After breakfast I record myself onto my mobile phone playing Clair de Lune, which now, after quite a lot of practice, I can do reasonably well, and send it to him, grinning into the camera (because smiling makes me look younger). I hope that makes him really, really sad and regretful; because I jolly well am. What a weak pathetic wanker. Best off that I have never actually met him, I comfort myself.

During the day I get annoyed by some idiot lost deliverer-woman who keeps phoning me for directions - why can't she just use her sat-nav like everybody else, and I don't remember having ordered anything anyway.

I come downstairs in the evening to find a large bouquet of flowers in one of those boxes, left sitting on my freezer. "Love Stephen" says the little card, written by the flower shop's receptionist in baby-script.

Yuck! How I hate flowers! They're always like this - always a sorry for a let-down. Symbolic only of disappointment, never joie de vivre. A pathetic waste of money, easy-peasy hope of getting let out of jail free.

Well not from me, mate. I don't throw them away. But don't put them in a large vase to show off in the hall either. They remain in their practical purple box, and I dump them on the kitchen table, wondering whether I ought to thank, comment, or what really.

So in the event I say nothing, and 24hrs later, I duly receive a tentative enquiry from Stephen as to whether I have binned them. I reply with both barrels of my normal reaction to flowers, suggesting that a cheque might have been more useful. And never expect to hear from him again.

Wrong!

He is clever.

He is apologetic, understanding, kicking himself, and has been bollocked by his very nice sounding daughter who rides about as enthusiastically and badly as I do (it would appear from a photo Stephen sent), and who, extraordinarily enough, saw me on Four In A Bed!

So we're back in contact again, and his emails are getting funnier and funnier! Could it really happen that I could become an item with a brummy who says things like "at the minute" and "I was stopping at"?

Sitting around a brazier shivering in a Hardyesque gathering of my mate Sarah's immediate community in her Dartmoor garden, a week or so later, I attempt to imagine 'my Stephen' being a part of the merry throng.

Sarah's husband of twenty-five years is a spy for the US, stationed only ever in the most dangerous parts of the world. I have seen a pic of him running along the street in Iraq, clutching a Kalashnikov. Some years ago he emerged top in his post-grad four year course of Arabic at Exeter University - even though there were actual Arabs on it. He is extraordinarily interesting, massively charming, good looking and funny. Yes. I think 'my Stephen' would definitely be able to hold his own...

Single Women Unite!
16/08/2016

"How would you feel if I suggested bringing my BBQ Party to yours?" queries Karen, my single Mum friend from Totnes. "Since the end of the family home; and the end of the joint rental now that Charles is history, my titchy terrace house just isn't big enough even for a small party, whether it's in the garden or outside," she says.

"I'd love you to bring your party here!" I enthuse. "But it will have to be in the field, or in the drive at the back of the house, or in the teenage Hell-hole, so that we don't disturb the B&Bers. And you will have to do everything because I am too tired, and too pissed off generally to have the energy to get behind it all with cooking, asking friends of my own blah blah.."

I hear nothing for a few days, and then a small voice, "I feel just the same as you actually.."

"OK, just you and me. Let's get pissed and moan, and you can stay the night," I suggest cheerfully.

So that's what we did. Only Karen is a pro at this, while I'm still an amateur. 'In my cups' I never really get beyond merry and chatty. I don't think I've ever fallen over through drink, and almost never slurred my words and hopefully haven't said things I regret, or worse, forgotten altogether what I've said. Perhaps I'm a control freak.

By the end of two or three bottles of wine, we both agree that our marital bust-ups don't seem to have panned out all that beneficially for anybody involved. Oh well. Not a lot to be done about it now. Boo hoo.

Time for bed.

Karen is bright in the morning, while I am totally out of it and prepare B&B breakfast in zombie mode; then off to meet Walter, Karen's ex-boyfriend who she's matchmaking me with today.

Wow!!! He's gorgeous! All dark hair and chiselled features and fit and muscular and warm and smiley and chatty. Yum. Yum. Yum! How could she have kept this a secret!

But. It turns out he has lived abroad for most of his adult life, and has never done a proper job. Now aged fifty, he allows Karen to pay for his lunch. Oh no. No, no, no. I'm not going through all that again. On to the next one...

No More Toffs
31/08/2016

Half an hour after I received Stephen's disappointing email I had my revenge. I signed up for three months with match.com. I'd had it with Encounters.

Match.com provides you with the facility to 'shuffle' through 100 tattooed labourers living within twenty miles of your home, so finding the quality chaps is a bit like rifling through TK Maxx's rails.

Eventually, numbed by people who like walking their dogs on the beach and cosy nights in on the settee, I came upon a potential life-partner calling himself 'Patriarch'. All I had to go on was that he lives in Sherborne (posh and brainy), he's a Leo (party animal), is 6'1" and 58 years old. No pic. No profile. 'Like' I pressed, and next thing I know, Patriarch - or rather, Adrian - has re-subscribed to the site, especially for me, says his long, jolly message.

"I am utterly delighted that you say ha! instead of the ghastly LOL. But you are probably hideous which would be a real bummer," I reply.

To which he sends me some pics, and blow me down, he's got hair! And in his early years bore a striking resemblance to Elvis! He was a money trader in the CIty, and is now semi-retired, helping his ex-wife run a cattery in Dorset. On the phone he is pure Sarf London.

"Well," I think to myself. "It's high time I ended all this privately educated classist bollocks."

While it's so much easier on first dates to converse with men from the same background as oneself, just where has it got me actually? Simply because they went to schools that I've heard of, and they know what not to wear and which words not to say, doesn't mean that they're stimulating, funny, sensual, or 'bien dans ses paux'. At school I used to sit behind rows and rows of boys, examining their haircuts and guessing which hairdresser in Windsor they frequented, wondering who I might be going out with next. Silently giving almost every one of them a 'non'. So why should these posho's (now bald, fat, and often disappointed) prove to be any better than anyone else, forty years on?

"The privately educated online dates are all emotionally damaged," I concluded, "and the nice ones are married."

So. I have now opened a whole new world to myself! Of people who didn't go to private school! Bring them on!

Sad
20/9/2016

"Hello,

The honest answer is that since you have forced me to think, somewhere along the line the 'spark' seemed to go and I'm not sure when exactly and why. I know you don't want to hear this, but I still like you a lot, but the intensity has ebbed. It's probably down to all my fannying around."

The final words from Stephen, who has stood me up, changed his plans, delayed, prevaricated - well I really can't count the number of times.

"Never try to pin down a Pisces!" screams the blurb on "How to date a Piscean" that I looked up on Google. So I didn't. Until finally, in total exasperation - I did. And this is the result.

Well bollocks to that. It's really not very kind. So I suppose I am well rid. And the endless days of waiting for him to finally appear, just once in four months, I have spent teaching myself sad tunes on the piano. I can now do some not bad renditions of Debussy's Clair de Lune; Chopin's Nocturne No 19; and Liszt's Liebestraum No 3. I have put them up on YouTube so that everyone can discover how romantic I am at heart. They all sound remarkably similar.

But along the Stephen journey I have experienced a tummy ache from disappointed misery a lot of the time, and with this email it's come back again.

Breathe. Relax. Swallow. Move on.

During all Stephen's prevarication, I met Adrian - having pre-warned him that my heart was elsewhere.

He turned out to be a real gentleman, with round shades and a necklace. He brought me a bottle of Chablis Premiere Cru as a present and paid for my lunch, and we exchanged stories about our drunken misspent youth in the City in the 80s. He is perfectly nice, but. What? I think he might be too thin for me. He almost chain smokes roll-ups which don't smell too bad, but I guess they keep the weight off. I had a nice big fish pie for lunch, while he was satisfied with just a tuna wrap.

And now, coinciding with being dumped by Stephen before anything had actually happened, I have two items of interest who have popped up on match.com. Both weigh over 16 stone! Hurrah!

One is very familiar with Dartmoor and is moving to Budleigh Salterton shortly. He is the unusual combination of spiritual and funny. We discovered that we were both skirting around each other on Encounters as neither of us had paid the subscription, whereas we each had a leftover sub on match.com and so are finally able to communicate. It was a great surprise to me when he popped up on there.

The other possibility is a widower from Truro. At the moment we are discussing all the varieties of poached eggs and hollandaise you can get, and how to get the hollandaise to stay on top of the egg instead of dribbling down the side of it. He has a masters degree, is a session musician, and also, clearly, a cook, as he knows considerably more about preparing the perfect breakfast than I do.

I might be able to seduce both of them with the written word, but I'm not convinced how much they'll like me in the flesh. I'm not half as spiritual and arty as I can make myself sound. And with all this grief my chocolate/Cava belly is ever-expanding.

My writing skills, if you can call them that, are not only handy in the online thing, but also I have just knocked up a Personal Statement for my 17 yr old son Will, in 90 minutes flat. Obviously I think it is completely brilliant. It starts with "When I was 10 I used to busk on my sax to the sheep outside our garden gate." Hah! That will get him noticed!

Rich Men
26/10/2016

As previously observed, if you press 'shuffle' on match.com, you get sent pictures of 100 men. That's 100 new chaps, aged 48 - 63, living within 100 miles of me, joining match.com, every day! All you have to do is press yes or no, on their face.

But the most amazing thing of all about this, is how I seem to press 'no' to every single one of them. Tattoos, short gelled hair, shaven heads, bald men, bearded men, fat men, thin men, black shirts, flowery shirts, wide ties, shiny suits, light tan shoes, t-shirts (or, even worse, vests) with writing on, necklaces, bracelets, mass-produced modern furniture in the background, cheap insubstantial doors with horrid door handles, naff ornaments on ghastly thirties fireplaces, neat rectangular suburban gardens, grinning holding up pints of beer - all get the 'non' treatment.

And on top of all of that, nine out of ten of them have been educated at 'some college' or 'high school' and they're called Stu, Dave, Pete, Shaun, Kevin, Derek, Steve, Wayne or Ken. A firm 'non' all.

Call me a snob. I can take it. It is my doom.

And anyway. So what. I have just had a complete and utter brainwave! I am so excited!

I have found the website's search engine and typed in: "Earnings: £75,000

- £175,000+" and "Education: bachelors degree/masters/PhD".

And guess what?! Up pop (17 out of 12,576) pictures of fit, well dressed, good-looking men, with witty, articulate, and original personal profiles! It's like coming across a hidden treasure trove after seven years of trying!

So I've whizzed off messages to about six of them. I am most interested in a bloke describing himself as 'Laconic' who, from his pictures, can't be, as he is clearly a racing driver. I wrote "What are you doing standing on Windsor Bridge?" to him, as that is a place of many very happy memories for me.

But now I have another worry. My decision to eat chocolate and drink Cava because nobody cares whether I have a big tummy or not has come round to bite me on the bum. If I ever manage to meet any of these highly attractive and almost certainly sought-after gentlemen, they won't like me because I'll be too fat.

Muddy Match?
7/11/2016

There's a pilot's jacket fresh from the dry-cleaners hanging off the door handle.

A smart lady with short hair and beautifully painted nails sits at the desk.

I am in the office of the Virtual Jet Centre, on the way home from my health club, just down the road from Amy's launderette in the titchy town of Chudleigh where I get my B&B bed linen washed and ironed.

I am here to meet an online date called Archie. He's not expecting me. About an hour ago he 'messaged' me via Muddy Matches, but I haven't subscribed to that one (yet), so I'm not allowed to read what he said, nor send a reply. So I thought I would just pop in on him at the centre where, in his profile he said he works, instead.

There's a Porsche 911 parked outside the industrial unit where his simulator-thing is housed, but unfortunately it's not his, as it turns out that he's away for the week. Bummer. I like the lady though, who is his PA, and luckily she is aware of his online dating habit. So I scribble her a note to read out to him, and sweep away, my recently blow-dried hair bouncing on my shoulders.

Five minutes after I get home the phone rings and it's him. We have so much in common it's ridiculous. His eleven-year-old daughter is also called Faye, and he's got two horses, like me. He says he's loaded with money. Well that's original! From the pics he could not be called classically good looking, and he says 'cheers', but I really like his direct approach and his niche, original, entrepreneurial and clearly successful business. His PA seems fond of him too.

Watch this space.

Oh by the way. None of my match.com rich men replied.

And the promising bloke from Budleigh Salterton turns out to have been living with his Mum on the North Circular in Enfield, and is now looking for a small flat to rent in Budleigh. Hmmm. Not really for me.

Serial Online Dater
1/12/2016

"haaa why should people get to know me?? err my be a tiny bit biest this!! But who else should i get to wright it? my mum? i dont think so ether.. get to know me because of a ****load of reasons and one of them been that you will be surprised and i tell you no lyes."

How refreshing! Someone saying it how it is, at last! I am tempted to send a message to the straightforward but uneducated 'fellny76' from Leeds, telling him so, but that would only lead to yet more fruitless email exchanges leading nowhere, wasting time for both of us, so I will resist.

Instead I am about to make a call to Charlie of Tavistock, who appears to be the only civilised erudite chap on the whole of match.com. That would be too good to be true - someone I actually like, living locally, so don't hold your breath.

In desperation, I am currently subscribed to four sites, as I recently joined 'Elite Singles', in a midnight moment of tipsy madness, simply because I had got so fed up with ticking in all of their useless irrelevant boxes, only to find at the end of 30 minutes of it, they were demanding £138 before I could go any further - so I coughed up for three months!

There was only one Elite Single who caught my eye - the most gorgeous pic of a chap from Bristol. I contacted him to discover that he was fly-fishing in Northern Spain, and a frenzied exchange of messages took place - so exciting! Until we spoke. Turns out he's a BT engineer for the police in Exeter. We did meet up for lunch at my Club and like most people - he was very nice. But he was never going to do it for me.

A day or two later I met up with Archie the pilot. By now I was beginning to become quite familiar with the Club's menu. Archie was very unhappy at being forced to eat amongst the old people and pretentious chandeliers of my lovely Club, as opposed to some beery hell-hole dive, and he really minded that the service was so slow, whereas I thought it was funny. And then he blamed my poor Club for a subsequent whole week of severe food poisoning. Odd, since we both had minute steak, which you can eat minced, raw, with tartare sauce, if you really want to, can't you? And anyhow, I was fine so it can't have been that!

A couple of days later I repeated the experience yet again, but this time with Mike, who sells old toys at fairs all around the country. He was off to buy a caravan off eBay after lunch.

Mike, it transpired, left school with no qualifications, became a builder, and then, aged 38, wrote to Bristol University applying to do a Law degree.

They invited him in for an interview, and then asked him to pass one A level. He took two - and became a lawyer! And now he sells old rocking horses and train sets - he showed them to me, all piled up in his big white van in the Club's car park.

He is in the middle of having all his teeth changed by Bristol dental undergraduates, so at the moment he has a couple missing which will be put back in February after the start of their Spring term.

He has a 21 yr old son who has a slot DJ-ing trance music (which sounds like a record being scratched and has no tune, harmony, nor words) at Boomtown, the coolest festival of all; and a daughter who provides merchandise for the biggest touring bands, some of whom occasionally stay the night on the floor of Mike's sitting room in Bristol.

"They don't drink or smoke, and insist on early nights these days," Mike sighed. "Because they now earn their money from touring, playing literally hundreds of nights a year, rather than from record sales - the RocknRoll life is over, and they need their sleep and their health."

Interesting bloke, Mike. His stepfather was Maggie Thatcher's chauffeur and bodyguard, and Mags would occasionally pop in for coffee unannounced at his mother's house in Rattery. She has an album of photographs of Maggie, including some pictures of her sunbathing on the beach at Polzeath, wearing white plimsolls.

"Really cool about your online date's son," wrote Will. "I think this date might be a keeper, because free backstage tickets would be a dream!!"

Much as I like Mike, who calls me 'Lovely Lady', I can't see it quite working. I think he would let me get away with being too bossy.

So. Right. I'm going to call Charlie. Perhaps he will prove to be The One!

Too Good To Be True
15/12/2016

Well there's this bloke.

Who I would be proud to be on the arm of, and to introduce to all my friends - as opposed to vaguely embarrassed by, as I would be about most of my other online dates.

The minute he gave me his email address of course I Googled him. What self-respecting girl wouldn't?

Well blow me down but he's an OBE! And an MBE! He's a magistrate and heads about a million committees, having worked in Intelligence in the army for thirty years, and having been a director of the biggest security company in the world (I knew its founder when it comprised just 15 people, 35 years ago. He was Professor of Politics at Exeter University and he used to visit our student cottage, delivering a basketful of plums and singing arias in a rather good tenor voice).

I mean blimey - this bloke is ultra-mega-brainy! Responsible! Grown up! Has probably saved 1,000s of lives! And he's funny and good looking and solvent too - and just the right age at 60. Trouble is he likes sailing in Scotland, and fell-running, and lives in a little miner's cottage in remotest Cumbria. People probably think I'm hearty just because I live in the middle of nowhere, but I haven't been for a walk in years, except to the pub. Well perhaps if he gets me a horse and a piano I could bear it there. All that rain and bleakness.

Anyway - at the moment he appears very keen, but we haven't even spoken on the phone yet, quite apart from meeting me and my Cava/chocolate belly, nor discovering that I am shallow, ignorant, lazy and hedonistic. I think he's in for a big disappointment.

My New Job
15/12/2016

"Hi it's Mark; I've paid the money into your account," said my answerphone.

Eh? Who? What? I deleted the message.

Going through the zillions of emails I receive every day - mostly spam from HomeandAway holiday rentals, or Allison's Tutorial Courses - I nearly rubbed one out, prior to reading it; and stopped.

It was from 'Mark' - telling me that he'd paid up-front for two online dating profiles to be written on him.

Aggghhh!!!! I'd completely forgotten about setting up that website - www.profile-writer.com! I couldn't remember what I'd said on it, or how I charged, or how much - or anything! And the website hosting thingy was due to run out at the end of this month anyway.

Well it turns out that I'm only charging £75 to write each of my potential customers' individual profiles. That's not enough when I'm starting from scratch and I'm busy. More agghhh!

So I ring the guy and it turns out that he wants profiles written about him for two different sites. And then, mmmmmmmmmmm - he sends a picture of himself - and he is drop dead gorgeous!!!

On top of which - it turns out that he's a multi-millionaire who drives a Ferrari, and snowboards and sandbuggies and.. and... and... Oh yes! He's also funny and charming on the phone. And then I discover that the profile he's written for himself is so good already that I can't improve upon it. I offer to reimburse him. And then discover the problem(s).

He's 48 and wants children. What to do?

Well, first we lie about his age. I put him in at 43, with his 44th birthday this week. And then we have to put 'yes' in the 'wants children' slot; and change his preferred age-range from 18 - 35; to 33 - 38. We also have to improve his chat-up lines. "Fancy dinner on Friday - here's my mobile number" simply isn't working.

I am completely addicted to sorting the whole thing out. I find that I am checking his dating sites every hour, and making little tweaks to his profile on each of them. We become good friends and he whacks me a further £150 for 'any extra expenses'.

I am imagining that he will be receiving 300 messages a day via Encounters, and be featured on the 'Most Popular' page.

But non. I have failed. Even if you're like James Bond in almost every way - being a man of 48 looking for a much younger model just doesn't seem to be quite working. Where have I gone wrong? Am I going to have to admit failure and reimburse him after all?

Too Good To Be True Indeed
23/12/2016

Oooh! Mr OBE/MBE has sent me an email during the night! I wonder what it says!

Ah.. it's his CV. A list of all his achievements over the past thirty years or so. But I've read about them already on LinkedIn.

I ask Faye "Do you think I could behave alright amongst important, serious people?"

"No." She says. "Actually yes." I kiss her blonde little head.

He is celebrating his 60th birthday at a posh London club tonight - 80 people for champagne and oysters. Backwards and forwards go our emails, we speak at last, and he has a beautiful voice and is lightly charming and funny.

I'm not sure he's ever got as far as Googling me, to find out who I am and what I'm actually like, though. Because he never asks anything about all the stuff that's on there about me, even though he now has my whole name.

I wish him a happy party five minutes before it's due to start, and he thanks me. Later I send a little message saying I hope it went well.

And I never hear from him again.

Every second of every minute of every hour for 48 hours. I am desolate. I can't think straight. I forget to shut the gate to the horses and they escape into the garden. I tip a cup of coffee onto my white bedspread. I am in pieces. I lie awake at night making up emails to punish him with.

Finally I have finessed the ultimate, ultimate Fuck Off You Dick email to him, and press 'send'. It reads: "R U OK?" Hah! That will get him!

By return he sends "Yes! I've just met somebody, and I can't run two people along at once."

I am so upset I forget to go to the only drinks party I've been invited to throughout the Christmas period. I am also trying to prepare for my own "House Re-Warming Party" for 60 locals; to celebrate the fact that I have now happily changed my mind and decided not to move after all, since the planned sale failed to materialise. But now it is with such a heavy heart.

My party seems jolly, but I am sad, still turning over brilliant put-down pros in my head. By 11pm my final email is burnished bright, and ping - off it goes. Two seconds later and the phone rings. It's him of course! We talk for two hours - late into the night!

All about him. I don't think he even questioned whether it might be inconvenient or embarrassing calling so late. He's much more interested about whether I'm a size 12 or 14, than whether I like living in Dartmoor or what I enjoy doing etc.

Eventually we part, and I go to bed feeling rather relieved it's all over.

Two Timing Bitch
6/1/2017

I feel terrible! I've never done this before - but at the moment I'm playing two men off against each other!

I spoke to them both on the same day last week, and have arranged to meet one for lunch in Cheltenham's 2 Michelin starred restaurant this

Wednesday; and the other, after a school 'forty years on' (agh!) reunion dinner, for lunch somewhere near Ascot on Saturday. I am nervous that I won't remember what I've said to each one, and will start repeating myself. The guilt! The guilt!

The Cheltenham one sounds rather rich and very clever, having successfully sold a software business many years ago, he's now a business consultant with clients around the world. The other one lives next door to Hickstead, runs a horse livery yard and has a sand school in his grounds, was educated at Cranleigh, and was nicknamed 'Jonafun' by Paul McCartney, who is a client of his Events business.

But I have had my comeuppance.

Now that the lunch dates have been set and we've had our phone chats, I can see that both men are continuing to log into Encounters, but neither has replied to my jolly phone-call follow-up messages.

Undeterred, yesterday I went shopping in the sales, and finally found three dresses that camouflage my ever-increasing Cava-cortisol girth. On arrival home, I ordered Faye to photograph me, looking thinnish, in front of the Christmas tree, and uploaded the result onto the Encounters site, to remind both potential life-mates of my various attractions.

Neither appears to have noticed.

Oh Help! Life's Gone Mad!
18/1/2017

He's just as delicious in real life as he is in his pics!

I'm feeling a little swirly and surreal, having finally retired the night before at 2am after attending my Old School Dinner, and in front of me is Jonafun. We're meeting for lunch in a large characterless pub in Lightwater, just off the M3, as I make my way home from my Alma Mater to Dartmoor.

Jonafun works with loads of big names, and he travels around the world to places like Abu Dhabi. Yesterday he sold a large house, and he's got loads of land he's hanging onto until planning permission is granted. He also plays cricket for the county veterans.

Finally - at long, long last - I have met somebody who makes me feel rather fat and inadequate. He is a fit, intelligent, interesting and interested, solvent grown up.

I can only manage half my moussaka, as I am so all over the place.

He's shortly off skiing, but would like to see me again early next week, on his way down to Cornwall.

Next stop is Faye's school where I'm to take her out for a McDonald's, and return her for a 2hr talk on horses, while I meet a second date, who calls himself 'Paragon' and sells backboxes for bicycles.

Paragon is just what it says on the tin - a good-looking, smartly turned out 68 yr old. Actually he looks ten years younger, but comes across as a bit hard and un-smiley for me.

My phone bleeps and it's a text from Faye saying, "This is boring."

"Concentrate!" I bark back, and get into my car to go and collect her.

I feel a bit odd. I've only had two spritzers and half a further small glass of white wine. I blow into the ever present breathalyser.

"Beep beep beep!"

Yikes! I've reached the limit! How did that happen? I've only ever managed to do that, that one time before! Well I say! The government's figures must be right after all - if you don't eat. I reach Faye's school OK but my oh my, that was scary!!!

Finally home, I absentmindedly click into hopeless useless Elite Singles, and, for once, there's a quirky message with no spelling mistakes, from someone called Geoffrey.

*"..Throw away the hair gel and printed tee-shirts I guess!!
That is a dilemma!
Can I make a suggestion that we have a chat on the phone tomorrow perhaps? I think it might be funny!"* he writes.

He calls me. He's travelled the globe sailing, knows my friend the world's leading naval architect, is a rally driver, and has homes in Majorca and on an isolated part of Devon's north coast. He's GORGEOUS in his pics! He's literally on his way to Majorca while speaking though - back early next week, when he would like to meet me.

I joined the site because two Devon-based friends have found love through it, but until now, for months there's been nothing on it but tiny pictures of fat men with tattoos and crew cuts who live miles away.

Yet all of a sudden, not only has Geoffrey popped up - Dick says he's coming to see me. Dick used to ride point-to-pointers at a stable just down the road, he played tennis for the Hurlingham Club, he was an underwriter at Lloyds, and now trades every morning from wherever he happens to be. He has already booked himself into Prince Hall Hotel for - guess when? Early next week!

Meanwhile Mr Cheltenham hasn't gone completely off the boil. He now says he wants to meet me some time in early Feb.

I'm drowning! Help!

And Then There Was One ...
26/1/2017

Dick booked himself into the Prince Hall Hotel for two nights.

Always a gamble that. Having taken one look at me, will he turn and run, like that last blind date who escaped before breakfast without paying for the second night?

Dick and I enjoyed a delicious luxury dinner of prawns followed by grouse and a plate of different chocolate things, accompanied by a bottle of Chablis, and a glass of Malbec each. Finally, by the time we retired to the bar for coffee, I was pissed enough to interrupt his flow. "And another thing...!" I ranted.

I think those were the first words I'd managed to get in, over the past five hours, as he told me all about every dog he'd ever owned, his children, his Mum, his wives, his jobs blah blah blah.

Finally I excused myself at midnight, and breathlysed myself I as I set off in my truck down the skiddy frozen lane.

"Hmmmm 0.05. Not too bad," I thought to myself, as I noticed the temperature gauge was reading -2C, and - whoopsadaisy! The car suddenly made the most enormous slew across the ice-covered lane to the left, nearly hitting the bank. Gently does it...

In our wellies, Dick and I set off the next day to explore War Horse Territory, hoping to bump into the local hunt in the wildest, bleakest most open expanse of southern Dartmoor. And blow me down we came across them straight away! About forty horses, ridden by so many of my greatest friends, racing across the top of the moor! There are few more beautiful sights.

Despite being a bit chatty, Dick is actually rather tall and good looking and well preserved for his 59 years and I was quite proud to introduce him to everybody, as they paused to say hello, mid-flight.

But I began to get that tummy-ache feeling of boredom, over our pub lunch, as he continued with more anecdotes, normally ending in how clever he'd been. After we'd found and explored that little house they filmed as the boy's farm in War Horse, I drove Dick back to his hotel.

Luckily my mate Carla joined us for a drink that evening to share the burden. He really is such a nice guy. I wrote and told him so. I said "Please promise me, with your next date, to ask her a question about herself once every thirty minutes?"

Meanwhile, not a whisper from lovely Geoffrey from North Devon, whereas gorgeous Jonafun has just popped up out of nowhere after two weeks, wanting to meet up somewhere nearby, next week. If he can still look good in trainers at 62, all is not entirely lost!!

What Goes Around Comes Around
15/03/2017

"Have you come across my Nemesis, man-eating-man-magnet-cant-ride-very-well-Tasmanian-She-Devil-blah-blah?" I enquire of a posh-looking bloke on Encounters who hunts, and is another one who turns out to have been taught by my father in his youth.

"Yes I had and I was warned about the Tassie Devil. ...but I think I'm safe now..." he replies.

Blimey - this is just some stranger off the internet who turns out to have come across Her! What must it be like to have a reputation like that, stretching so far and wide!

This potential date appears to be a bit grand and rather old for me, but could be a bit of a laugh, and we clearly have loads of mutual acquaintances. I keep pushing, but he doesn't appear to be all that responsive. I am becoming increasingly suspicious that a disappointingly large proportion of the chaps online are simply dipping their toe in the water to see what happens, and aren't actually seeking a committed relationship at all.

Gad Zoosk!
25/4/2017

Yet another loved-up couple holding hands over my breakfast table. I am so jealous. Why can't it happen to me?

I've had loads of guests who tell me they met online. These two succeeded using something called Zoosk!, which I've never heard of.

So in a tipsy midnight moment, Jonafun never having come back to me, I find myself signing up, £54 for six months.

I am immediately inundated with messages from the up-all-night brigade, so in despair I write a profile designed to keep them at bay:

"I'm really sorry and call me judgmental, but I don't really do beards, tattoos, flowery shirts, vests with messages on them, cheap doors, gelled hair, thick soled or pointy shoes, abbreviated names, spelling mistakes, LOL, walking on beaches with dogs at sunset with every other lonely heart in the entire world, or men who are looking for 'a lady'. That would be almost everybody on this site, then. Oops."

But the wink's and the messages and the views and nods just keep on flooding in. And then, amongst them all, comes a witty message from a bloke just down the road in Buckfastleigh. He's filled in his profile under the 'Perfect Match' heading:

"A 'perfect match' would be one that strikes first time in damp weather."

Now that is my kind of humour. Back and forth our messages flow until I write: "I'm actually 57. How old are you really?"

It turns out he's 75 and called Keith.

Back to the drawing board.

The Perfect Man
10/5/2017

"I know the perfect man for you - Richard!" cries Angela, in her lilting Scottish brogue.

Angela and Sophie, fellow school Mums - also divorce victims who are now forced to run B&Bs and holiday rentals to make ends meet - have driven over from Somerset to inspect my new posh B&B, after I've spent three months and £20,000 on dragging it upmarket, and to submerge themselves in the hot tub.

"Not Richard Lewis!" I exclaim. "He owns that horse out there in my field! He's one of my best mates! But I'm not sure I would ever go out with him - I'd eat him for breakfast!"

Small world - it turns out that Angela once had a date with him, via Encounters, a few years ago. And on paper, of course, Richard and I make a perfect match - hence the reason why we're such good friends, probably.

Next to Angela I am fat, humdrum and unextraordinary. She is tall, fit, slim and vibrant; she lets out her holiday rental for twice what I get for Wydemeet; and she jumps proper massive hedges on her 17.2hh mare; she hosts bashes for people like Shirley Bassey and Pierce Brosnan, and is now in a long term loving relationship with an MBE naval bloke. She is really cool and I am vastly impressed by her.

I can't wait to tell Richard about my new best friend.

"Missed a trick there, didn't I?" sighs Richard.

Fuck
20/5/2017

"You don't seriously live in a village called Fuck do you?" I messaged an online date whose username is GenuineMileage.

And guess what. He didn't reply.

And then a few months later, he did. So I coughed up my £28.80 fee to re-subscribe to Encounters, and our correspondence commenced.

Yesterday I spoke to him on the phone, and he made me laugh.

He had a nice posh voice, used to be a lawyer in China, has written a thriller called 'Birds' Nest Soup' which currently lies at 4,803,201 in the Best Sellers chart on Amazon (even lower than my first book) and is now finalising a screenplay with a view to making a film in Elstree. He was at school with Jeremy Clarkson, and resides at the family home with his sister and her son, somewhere in Cornwall, south of Truro, in a village called Feock.

Well he's got an old friend from China coming to stay for a few days, called, no, not Chang; he's called Pete. I said I would be game to meet both of them for a coffee (I didn't say I'd much rather lunch or dinner), and now I'm waiting to hear when.

I'm a bit worried because on the thing it says he's 51, and with a username like his, that's probably true. So he's young enough to go out with girlies of 45; whereas I put that I was 54 when I'm actually 57, with an extremely crinkly wrinkly torso, fat floppy tummy and greying thinning hair (except on my chin, where it appears to be getting thicker). But I won't worry too much because I don't suppose he'll ever call back anyway.

Meanwhile.

The doorbell rang yesterday, while I was in the middle of serving my very nice American couple breakfast. I love these guests because they like having breakfast at 10am, which means that I can have breakfast in bed myself, before preparing theirs.

Anyhow I went to answer the door, in my apron, and standing on the step was an ancient old bloke with bad teeth, wearing horrible shoes and an anorak. He must have been about 80.

He took one look at me, and blanched.

"Keith," he stuttered. "You said I could pop round anytime."

"Well I'm in the middle of doing B&B breakfast," I retorted.

He turned and went away.

BACK ON THE SHELF

6 LOVE IN THE COUNTRY

WHAT'S A STALKER LIKE?
6/1/2017

To an accompaniment of Beethoven's Pastoral, Vivaldi's Spring, 'Loving You is Easy', or various sentimental Elvis tracks, Flash Gordon continues to pen (or email) me moving poetry via daily eCards.

"Sex Goddess!
Your lips are so soft and red, the thought of kissing you is in my head. Your beauty so bright and warm, shining through the darkest storm! xxxx"

" Lady Mary
A kiss is just a kiss until you find the one to love, A hug is just hug until you find the one you're always thinking of. A dream is just a dream until it comes true, Love was just a word until the day I met you. xxx"

Gordon is my most loyal admirer, and today we celebrate our first wedding anniversary.

He has read my first book over and over, watches me playing the piano on Youtube ('Mary Playing the beginning of The Moonlight Sonata in a Coat' has received 50 views!), and he's now been on the phone to the producer of Four In A Bed three times, for an hour each time, berating her because they appear to have taken down my episodes on Channel 4 Catch Up - after all that:

" Hi Sexy.

Have just spoken to the production team at Channel 4 to see if there's any exciting news in the pipeline about getting you and delightful Faye on gogglebox.

I spoke to the head of productions fuck-face Fiona and told her you had just spent 10 Grand on a yellow sofa from Harrods and was awaiting a delivery before Christmas in anticipation of getting on the programme with your lovely daughter Faye! She said there were hundreds wanting to get on the show I said yes but theres only one Mary and she's irreplaceable! and would be an ideal replacement for Steph and Dom the posh couple who have now left the show.

I told her you both live in mansions and are extremely funny with a spiffing sense of style and wit!

Also told her you would be great Eye Candy for all the male viewers who watch the show! She said she thinks I'm great! and i said if I'm that fucking great get them on your show Fiona baby so we are keeping in touch with each other. Lots of love Gordon xxxxx"

FOUR IN A BED AGAIN
2/2/2017

Look what arrived in my in-box a couple of days ago:

"Hello,

I'm writing on behalf of a TV production company called Studio Lambert and we are making a brand new series of Channel Four's popular TV show 'Four in a Bed'.

As you may know, we are looking for enthusiastic owners/managers, with a minimum of three guest bedrooms, who are willing to get behind their business and to share what makes their accommodation special. It is a brilliant opportunity for owners to not only showcase their property but also their local area and some of the delights it has to offer." blah blah blah

I was so angry at their poor research; this person not only unaware that Wydemeet had already been featured once, but also, after two weeks of my valuable time being dedicated to their show, our episodes being suddenly removed with no explanation provided; that I couldn't think quite how to reply. So I turned to Flash for advice:

"to flashgordonnot.
What shall I do about this???!!!!!"

to me

"Hello Sexy. I think you should take up this offer to go on this brand new series of Four in a Bed. It will be great to showcase your business and what you have to offer your guests ! Which is special accommodation in a fantastic location! And of coarse a beautiful host ! I have read all your reviews from your guests and they all love sexy Mary! When I rang Channel 4 and spoke to fuck face Fiona about getting you on Gogglebox I said you were made for television as you are attractive and
have a great personality sexy and Hilarious ! And she agreed also that you are a sexy beast and would make television worth watching!

Just think if you are on this new series you would be full every night especialy with men!!! The rest would be sitting at home on there yellow sofa dribbling in there Calvin Kleins undercrackers
watching sexy mary on tele !!!! Love Gordon xx"

So I did as he advised:

"Dear Four In A Bed Team

Many thanks for inviting me to take part in Four In A Bed again. I thoroughly enjoyed myself last time.

I am massively disappointed, though, that after devoting two weeks of my life to the show, in anticipation of its many re-runs, you have taken my episodes (Series 9 Episodes 1-5) off catch-up, with no explanation provided other than 'some issues regarding compliance'.

I believe my friend Gordon has already spoken to Fiona at some length about this, and I really do think that I am justified in feeling that I am owed an explanation of what these issues are. Access to my episodes was proving extremely helpful as a sort-of potted CV for potential online dates, which is the reason why I took part in your programme in the first place; as well as for help with the marketing of my B&B, which I feel was really rather part of the original deal.

So yes. I will take part again please, if you cannot resurrect my original episodes.

Thank you so much for the offer, and I very much look forward to hearing from you again soon.

With best regards

Mary Hadow (nee Nicholson)"

So we will see. I wonder whether they will even bother to reply.

GETTING OUT THERE
1/3/2017

"Hi Mary.

I have been in contact with Channel 4 and told them they are a bunch of fucking morons for not getting back to you. After all, they asked you if would like to take part in there programme, and after much thought you agreed. I told them you had a very successful business that was full to capacity most nights, and you would be doing them a service letting the crew film there again.

I also said I was raising a petition called " bring back Mary " to our televisions and already had over a thousand signatures, mainly from men, but was hoping to get more before sending it to CEO of Channel 4 David

Abraham.

You would have thought at least they could acknowledge your email even if they said " fuck off ". PS Of coarse I'm in love with you but I care about you as well. Gordon xx"

I arrived back to my delightful stalker Gordon's email from a "Ladies' Lunch", held by Faye's school, at which the speaker was a very successful author called Amanda Prowse. Apparently her books account for 10% of all Kindle sales. Well if you bear in mind that there are over 2 million books available on Kindle, that's a lot of sales - 100,000 a week, or something.

Anyhow I waited til I was last in the book-signing queue of her latest novel "The Perfect Daughter" (I have one of those already) and had a bit of a chat; and she was very serious about me sending her a copy of my books to take a look at. Ooh – I wonder what she'll think?

THE BEGINNING OF THE REST OF MY LIFE?
3/4/2017

"from feed merchants in Tavi" emails Richard, my great mate who I ride (horses) with, who Angela says is the perfect man for me, and he attaches a mobile phone pic of the following handout:

"The producers of Escape to the Country are currently searching for single people of all ages looking for love, but struggling because of their demanding country lifestyle or isolated location. An exciting new TV series for a major broadcaster, which will have singletons finding partners willing to give country life a go in return for the chance of love.

"If this sound like you, or someone you know, get in touch with our casting team at CountryLoving@ boundlessproductions.tv. What have you got to lose?"

So of course I do get in touch with them. Immediately. Even though I'm supposed to be meeting Catherine at Mount Kelly's new 50m swimming pool - the original warm-up pool from the London Olympics – at 2pm. Which, at £3 a dip, is so much calmer and more serene, never mind nearer, than any of the posh expensive health clubs I've belonged to in the past.

When, a couple of hours later, I arrive back at the chaos that is my home - somebody delivering logs, Matthew the electrician putting in new towel rails but failing to fit my expensive, bathroom-friendly chandeliers because of Wydemeet's ancient wiring - me having collected my horse trailer which I've had washed for £140 because, on display in my smart new yard it is letting down the new, upmarket tone that is Wydemeet; I am not at all surprised to discover that researcher, Liz, from the programme, has called by return.

I had told them that I am a posh single mother of teenagers living in the remotest B&B in southern England, the only males within a five mile radius having four legs and being covered in wool. "Come and film me mowing the lawn in my swimming costume and wellies," I suggested to them. I call Liz back.

"Can we send someone round to get some nice photos next week?" says Liz.

"I'm not convinced that 'nice' photos will be possible, but I'm fairly free next week," I reply.

"What are you looking for in love?" she queries.

"Someone for whom I would want to get in my car and drive over to see for supper, in preference to sitting on my own watching Britain's Got Talent with a Birds Eye frozen roast platter for one on my lap" I respond.

COUNTRY LOVING
8/4/2017

"Actually, could you make it tomorrow?" the telly people said.

So here we are! I've washed my hair, and put on my favourite top, which is a Phase 8 grey and white jumper/shirt combo from eBay. I am relieved it appears to have survived its first wash reasonably OK, but it's rather uncomfortable as it's still wet, and I hope it doesn't matter that I'm not going to iron it. The look is completed with black leggings, and high heeled black suede boots that I would never normally wear at home, but which make my legs look longer.

Kay is a really friendly person, just like all the 'Four In A Bed' people were, as is the cameraman, who looks like a sort of gulp-worthy Adonis. He must be 6'3", lean and fit in beautifully cut jeans, grey hair, a neat beard (beard? Agh! But even that is OK on this man) and a calm, smiling face.

They anticipate staying the entire afternoon, the sun is bright, and I settle into verbal diarrhea.

The programme is 'in development' for BBC2. The production company is behind 'Escape to the Country' and 'The Farmer Needs a Wife', amongst many other things that you would have heard of.

'In development' means that they have been funded to plan, research and film the beginnings of the series that they want to make, so I expect it will probably go ahead. Whether, if so, they'll want to come back and film me all over again, as they did for 'Four In A Bed', I don't really know. I haven't told them that I did 'Four In A Bed' in case that puts them off.

They film me chatting with a backdrop of Bellever Tor behind me, feeding the horses (which means I have to take off my heels and look fat in wellies), dusting the B&B room with a pink feather duster, tapping away on my laptop for my next book, and playing the piano to show my 'soft' side. It just couldn't be better PR for everything that I try to do. I become increasingly relaxed and start gesticulating wildly.

"And how would you feel about getting a partner?" they query.

"Well look at all of this beauty!" I cry, waving my arms around. "What is the point? All on your own? I come down from the field and see my wonderful home and I think 'why?' when there's no one to share it with! I might as well just be dead!"

The melt-in-your-mouth cameraman smiles at me in a protective, loving way, and discusses his wife and family. Then he shows me some footage taken by his drone, of the front of Wydemeet and then zooming in on the remote glory of the moor behind, and says that whatever happens, he will send it to me for use on my B&B website. So at least something will come out of all this - hurray!

Then he shows me the stunning shots he has taken earlier that day, of Dartmouth.

"Ahhh - that will be James. The one I met in the pub who, quite openly looked at his watch in front of me, and rushed off without pudding or coffee!" I say helpfully. That would be funny if they tried matchmaking me with him again.

Who Cares Anyway?
23/5/2017

What is it about me that puts the chaps off, with my lively, erudite, friendly pros??

So Genuine Mileage has gone silent; the hunt bloke is less than interested, and even a chap, from Zoosk, down the road, who's got long hair, a bit of a gut, says LOL and your instead of you're; and who wears a bracelet, hasn't got back to me. How dare they? Do they know what they're missing? NON! But my B&Bers do. If in doubt, just take a little look at my 95 tripadvisor reviews.

Anyhow - who cares. Because I'm going to be on telly again.

Kay rang yesterday and 'Country Loving' on BBC2 is definitely going ahead, she says. And guess who will be starring in it? Moi!!! Hah! So you can bugger off, all you ungrateful online losers. Be sad, be very sad!

ONE AND HALF MINUTES OF FAME
5/6/2017

Kate's lower lip trembles and her eyes well up.

"I can't do this, I keep on crying!" she wails.

We're sitting in the kitchen surrounded by lights and cameras, and she's supposed to be describing what I'm like as a friend, to the Country Loving telly people.

The trouble is, unusually for Reality TV, this is supposed to be an upbeat positive jolly sort of programme, so for once they don't want tears.

"She's such a good friend," sobs Kate.

I help myself to another piece of cake.

We have been filming now for about five hours, and I am astonished and touched that Kate has volunteered to take part.

"I've got millions of friends, and I can't think of a single one who would want to go on telly just for the sake of it," I said to the producers, when they sprung the need to get someone to talk about me on air. But when I mentioned this to Kate the other day, she immediately offered herself for the role, bless her.

And anyway, it's turning out to be fun! For both of us. Between tears, we're howling with laughter, looking at all my potential online suitors.

The telly people wanted to film me in the most romantic spot of all around here - at the confluence of the Swincombe and the West Dart; and also get some footage of me riding the horses; but we've had some hurricane wildly raging outside all day, with no sign of abating, so that's out of the question, sadly. I can't allow my hair to get wet or I look like Esther Rantzen, and I want to keep my high heels on, ensuring my legs look longer.

"What do you most miss about not having a man?" they pry gently.

"Ummm, errrrrr, weeeeell, I don't think the answer to that one would be suitable for a family show," I end up lamely.

What I have only recently realised is that this could become really, really big. To find potential dates for me, they plan to promote Country Loving on other BBC programmes, such as The One Show. There will be ten lonely hearts, or 'contributors', altogether, with our videoed profiles up on the BBC website. I can't believe that after all this mega-effort, each profile will be cut down to just 90 seconds!

But I think these other BBC programmes will want to parade us live; the 'romantic encounters' will presumably be filmed - and if all goes well, I anticipate papers like the Daily Mail doing features on us, researching our family backgrounds etc, like they do with I'm a Celebrity and Big Brother contestants. We could become national characters - like the people on Gogglebox!

Ooo-errrr. I wonder whether the other participants have realised all this, and whether they're brave enough to go through with it?

While I'm at it, who ARE the other participants?

"Have you got an OAP?" I query. "What about a proper ooo-arrrrr Devonian farrrrrrmer? How do you get someone like that to come up with endless soundbites? Have you got people of loads of different ages and backgrounds? What happens if the plan goes slightly wrong and the contributors start going off with each other, like Lance Gerrard-Wright did with Ulrika Jonsson in 'Mr Right' back in 2002?"

Well I am braced. I am bored. It's time for a new adventure. If I am to become a household name - good. It could open many doors, and certainly help with selling my books!

We've been here for five hours, we are drained, and it's time to wrap.

"What Mary really needs is somebody with an equal lust for life," concludes Kate, pulling herself together and giving the camera a broad grin.

I Am The Very Model Of A Modern...
5/6/2017

Meanwhile, 'Jaded of Dartmoor' has become so disillusioned with the whole online dating thing that I've changed my profile yet again, in the vain hope that the only messages I'll receive will be from people who absolutely get my sense of humour. I've put the following up on Encounters:

About her
My role is that of a life enhancer - to leave people more cheerful than they were when we met.

At the moment my life is ridiculously pleasurable. I swim, ride out across wildest Dartmoor, share elevenses, lunch, tea and/or dinner with mates, watch my two children play in concerts and on the sports field, and sing and play the piano to myself. I am financially secure living in a large house in central nowhere, running a successful B&B, within a thriving community I've known for twenty years. Lovely family, lots of holidays, visits to London, sailing, skiing ...

About her ideal match
So where are you? Doing the same somewhere else? Why haven't our paths crossed? Are you, too, slightly lonely, and looking for a principled, open, warm, quirky (but far from bonkers), un-clingy, stimulating soul mate?

I have had to be self-reliant throughout my eventful life, but would so love to feel looked after for once. Nobody has managed it yet. Could that person be you? Oh what fun we would have!

But there's a problem, and this is how it goes. I've turned it into a song of *the Gilbert & Sullivan genre. You see, I struggle with:*

Verse 1:
Facial hair; flowery shirts; vests with messages; and tattoos;
Black shirts; necklaces; bracelets; and shiny pointy shoes
Cheap doors; gelled hair; silly hats: trainers; and crepe soles
Shortened names, spelling errors, bad grammar; and cliches

deep breath

Verse 2
'LOL'; 'amusing'; 'humorous' and emojis;
'Lady', OAPs, and skinny health freaks;
Long white hair, lonely hearts and dogs strolling on the beach;
And 'cuuuuuuddles on the setteeeeee'.

oh, and possibly soccer. Oh and men with cats; and mass-produced furniture...

Errrr... anyone left?

Well guess what - I've been contacted by a retired army officer from Yeovil. The trouble is, he's only a major and I would prefer a Major General with letters after his name ...

Fascinating Woman
7/6/2017

That's what the bloke from Zoosk who has finally got back to me, called me.

Well - who could not be flattered?

He lives down the road. He's 54, 6'4", nicely dressed, fit, and drives a new 4-door Porsche which cruises down the A38 at 165mph (shame it's purple), and a Series 2 Land Rover. He has a sweet, shiny little black shooting spaniel, and he fishes the best rivers in Scotland. He sells scaffolding and equipment for oil drills around the world. He was brought up in five different countries, moving around with a non-commissioned father in the army, he's a Geordie, and wears a silver necklace as well as a bracelet. I can smell that he smokes, and indeed he describes himself as a 'social smoker' on Zoosk; and he doesn't drink. We're meeting at The Two Bridges for coffee, and we chat a lot about Top Gear and our mutual hero, J Clarkson.

After our meeting, I email him to say how refreshing it is to meet someone who's both interested and interesting; and that although we come from totally different worlds, I would like to meet again. This telly thing could prove to be a bit of a spanner in the works though.

I return home to a second email from the ex-master of our local hunt. He now lives in Bristol, and, although this time he's come via 'Muddy Matches', I've seen his profile before, on Encounters. We have my bonkers mate Jack as a great friend in common. Jack has clearly told 'Masterofthehunt' that we're made for each other, as he's invited us both out carriage driving on Monday; followed by dinner at his new place outside Totnes.

I've a feeling that I've already met this chap a few years ago through Jack, and if I've got the right one, he's jaw-droppingly handsome, and wears extremely smart, expensive brown hunting boots.

Oh Ho, What's This?
9/6/2017

Yesterday, a largish bloke called Ben turned up at Wydemeet, in a black Skoda estate.

I'd already had a two hour telephone conversation with him a couple of days earlier, and anticipated a typical, pleasant, going-nowhere encounter, just like nearly all the last 70 or so others I've had, dragging out over the past eight years.

The phone had been going so mental that morning that I didn't have time to bother with a bath, and I hadn't washed my hair for two days.

Anyhow, Ben got out of his car and he was just my type.

Smiley, stocky, slightly unkempt, ex-rugby player.

He arrived on the dot of 12.30pm as promised.

We shared a cafetiere of coffee. Chat chat chat. Then we drove to the pub, rather than walking, because we're still in the middle of some hurricane. Chat chat chat; including me admitting that I'm actually 57 (he's 51); and that I'm due to be on this lonely hearts telly programme thingy. I had two Spritzers and he had two pints of beer, and finally Roger the barman asked us to leave. By now it was an hour after closing time.

More coffee back home in the kitchen? I can't remember. Then he made me put on some wellies and go for a walk. I showed him the Fairy Bridge and gestured towards where Tinkerbell used to live.

"Oh yes, there she is," he said.

Eh? She got washed away in a flood, years ago - all that was left were her feet.

I peered into the nook, or is it cranny, under the bridge and OMG - she's come back!!!! So SWEEEEEEET!!!! So pretty!!!! About 3" tall. I can't wait to tell the children! Faye has recently taken to going the Fairy Bridge, in her running kit and earphones, and dancing to herself. She'll love to know that Tinkerbell is back, watching her!

Anyway - Ben and I turned round and walked home and had even more coffee, before my B&B guests were due to arrive.

Agh! They were early!!! So the four of us sat around the kitchen table tucking into rather nasty Tesco lemon drizzle cake.

Finally, at nearly 7pm, Ben said it was time for him to leave. He had been with me by now for nearly seven hours!

I stood an arm's length away as he sorted out getting into his car. I knew we could have gone into a full snog right out there in my drive, under the guests' noses, on our first meeting. But this was far too much for me to compute. Nobody's touched me for years!

Why on earth, of all the millions and millions of single men I have met through all the multifarious wretched online dating sites, over years and years and years, should this man, who does not obviously stand out immediately, outstandingly, head-and-shoulders above all the others, be 'the one'?

He's not particularly rich nor well-connected; he's reasonably good looking but no model; he's not particularly successful nor ambitious; not fantastically well-dressed; not obviously a charismatic leader of men; and he's most definitely not smooth.

Most importantly to me, because I am so shallow, what might my family and friends make of him, after all I've put myself, and them, through, over the past nearly-decade?

Is it that he's so comfortable to be with, and smiley, and clearly gentle and kind and chatty and a bit of a maverick, and writes, and lives down the road, and refuses to be employed by anybody else, and ran a B&B in his 20s, and went to the same school as Stephen Fry, and is six years younger than me?

He's not really what I had in mind....

And yet... And yet...

What did I actually have in mind? Somebody who could make me happy, was it? Somebody who's not so far up their own arse that I find myself lonely in my own home? Somebody who is actually kind to me? And who weighs more? And who makes me feel comfortable, secure, happy, proud of myself, loved? In short - somebody who will enhance my life?

And what am I going to do about the telly thing if I pursue this? Bloody hell what do I do now? I am suddenly in a blue funk. Dazed, confused, and actually, now that there is a real living, breathing, potential 'keeper' right in front of me, rather than some fantasy, I'm beginning to feel panicky. Ooo-er. My head is really spinning!

But I think I might be having a sort of sixth sense about this one...

And as if that wasn't enough, Vegas, Faye's horse, has just spectacularly failed the vet so I can't sell her.

And I woke up (at dawn this morning - my guests wanted breakfast at 8.30am, agh!) to discover that 40% of the British public appears to have voted for that wazzok Jeremy Corbyn. Has the world gone completely lala?

After sorting breakfast, I drove a 100 mile round trip to hear beloved Faye perform Radiohead's "I'm a Creep" in her school's 'Lunchtime Concert', and then did a quick mow of our storm bedraggled garden between hurricanes. I trimmed 'That Mad Fucker' (the horse)'s tail, avoiding being kicked and bitten; I've just had a hot tub; and finally retired to bed with a bottle of Cava at 5pm, having been unable to concentrate on anything properly, other than Ben, for the entire day. Be still my befuddled mind!

Drop Dead Gorgeous
29/6/2017

After saying goodbye on our first date, Ben and I had arranged our second meeting to take place a few days later, at his home in Sidmouth, a couple of miles on from The Double Locks pub where I was having lunch first, with some girlfriends.

What I hadn't told him about was Monday's carriage driving date with Drop Dead Gorgeous Donald the Hunt Master.

This turned out to be one of the most memorable and, on the face of it, potentially romantic evenings of my entire life. Donald and I arrived at Jack's at the same time - Donald in his work-clothes, having driven direct from his office in Bristol.

He looked delicious, but quickly changed into his equally attractive country attire, remarking how unhappy he was about the size of the letters saying 'Hunter', on the front of his wellies.

"Ah," I thought. "You don't get to be that good-looking without trying rather a lot!" For it was indeed the edible bloke I'd met a couple of years ago. He was slim and fit and could easily have got away with saying he was 40, rather than 51. I felt fat and squat, and very self-conscious, next to his 6'3" lean athletic frame; and I hadn't brought proper rural gear with me. My black poncho looks stupid with wellies.

Even worse, we were then ordered to put on a riding hat - immediately squashing what's left of my glorious blonde locks which I had gone to so much trouble blow-drying an hour previously. The hideous 'hat hair' look.

We set off in Mad Jack's coach-and-two at a gallop, lurching across his sunlit valleys behind two 17 hand powerful bay Gelderlanders - very smart Dutch driving horses. Donald's and my hands touched.

Having survived that - oh what fun! - Jack then ordered us into a little dinghy on his man-made lake, for Prinks; and as the sun set behind the hill in the distance, we shared champagne as Donald prepared steaks on the barbecue.

We ended the evening sitting around the fire-pit, with Jack racing around bringing anything we needed from his Range Rover; meanwhile Donald, having placed one arm protectively around my shoulders, was massaging my thigh beneath the warm woollen rug we were sharing.

I mean honestly! Nobody has touched me like that for at least four years!!!!!! It just felt weird!!

I resisted all his entreaties for me to stay the night with him in the luxury caravan, nestling under the moon and stars, in the valley by the lake; so reluctantly he walked back with me to my car, clearly urgently wanting to deep-kiss me, as we said goodbye.

Agh! Ben! Ben! Ben! I turned, and stiffened, and mumbled, "I'm so sorry but I can't respond, I'm afraid, because I've got this telly thing coming up...." and fled.

Overnight Stay?
29/6/2017

"Don't feel you need to come back from his house tonight - we can manage on our own in the name of lurve," offer my kind B&Bers.

Ben and I are sitting on a bench together, not touching, on top of a cliff, gazing out across Lyme Bay, a clear blue sky above us; a runner with a perfect body racing up and down the long steep hill from our vantage point to the beach below and back again, as she trains for the Three Peaks Race.

I confess to Ben what had and hadn't happened the night before.

Why have I suddenly gone from nought to six million, with two gorgeous men, plus the carrot of the telly series dangling in front of me, all at once, after literally years in the desert?

We return for tea at Ben's neat home on the outskirts of Sidmouth. He's bought me a little cake especially. And later we move on to supper - of ready-meal lasagne. He's got a bottle of Sauvignon for me in case I decide to stay, but he clearly hasn't made any assumptions about dinner. I am relieved, and touched. He says he would like to kiss me.

Afterwards, we sit on the sofa gazing out into the garden, holding hands.

"I'd better get back to my B&Bers," I mutter. "Might you come to my house tomorrow?" One more kiss and I struggle up to leave.

OMG.

Prepared
29/6/2017

He's brought the remains of yesterday's cake.

He's also brought his swimming trunks in case we decide to use the hot tub.

And his toothbrush.

Goodbye To All That
29/6/2017

"You have just ruined the rest of my life."

I look up at him, with a wide grin, as he emerges through the kitchen door for breakfast.

"I have done the deed."

By which I mean that I have said goodbye to all my hopes and dreams and excitement at the idea of becoming a famous and successful author, by PR-ing myself via the TV lonely hearts thingy.

And that's after they've made two visits to my house, and spent ten hours filming me. It was a very hard phone call to make, but I've managed it. They were remarkably sanguine. I would have gone absolutely mental if I were them!

Yet I've only met Ben three times. What a decision! But the telly people had left a message asking me to call them, and I cannot live a lie. Agh!

Perhaps if the programme's successful, and my new romance goes belly up like all the others, I can have another go in Series 2.

Pub Crawl
29/6/2017

"I'm visiting Mum today, but can I see you on my way back, tomorrow?" I beg.

So we meet for lunch at the Double Locks - my second sunny summers' lunch there in a week!

"Do you know the Turf Inn?" I query.

"Yes, I cycled there once. It's just down the towpath - shall we go on a pub crawl?" he suggests, as neither of us wants to go home yet, and it's still only lunchtime.

EIGHT MILES LATER!!! and I am knackered. It's bloody boiling! I'm feeling out-of-it from fatigue. He's offered to get the car from the Double Locks and come back to collect me, but I'm buggered if I'm going to be that pathetic. Anyway - it's turned out to be a really, really lovely day.

Party! Party!
29/6/2017

He's in London getting pissed at a family party; I'm in Portsmouth at an extraordinary 60th birthday party celebration in the Mary Rose Museum.

It is stunning - £26 million has been spent on producing the most beautiful, exciting, interesting, inspiring, interactive museum possible; but most of all I am thrilled to be among so many childhood friends of nearly sixty years ago - so warm and huggy and loving and kind.

He arrives the next day at my house for lunch at 1pm precisely, bearing gifts of home-made mackerel pate, salads and cheeses which we enjoy in the beauty of Wydemeet's garden. A real treat to be so warm on highest

Dartmoor. Then we repair to the river, where we sit for four hours together, chat chat chat chat chat.

Hot tub time and supper. I could get used to this! How long is he going to stay? I am free for the whole week, and he's promised to drive me to the hospital tomorrow for a yucky appointment which might involve a full anesthetic!

My my it's hot

Surreal
29/6/2017

Five days of uninterrupted total pleasure with this new man who has popped up out of nowhere. We've used Wydemeet as it's supposed to be used, in daily temperatures of 80+F. We have the house all to ourselves - no B&Bers staying, during the most beautiful Dartmoor June I have ever known in twenty years! What were the chances of that?!

We've developed our own little private, daily routine, of admin in the morning, lunch in the garden, and sitting in various parts of the river in the afternoon, followed by the hot tub and supper, and even more chat; familiarising ourselves with my two refurbed luxury B&B rooms which, now they are so very newly redecorated, and de-cluttered of any personal effects, feel like going on a luxury holiday in my own home. It is all so properly, genuinely romantic, surreal, and sheer bliss.

Why do I prefer my stocky Ben in his sloppy old t-shirts, ancient trainers, man-made-fibre jackets, and short, heavy, old, black wellies, to super-sleek Donald?

Because I think he's happy in his own skin. He's nothing to prove. He is what he is, which makes him powerful and, finally, almost impossible for me to expose and emasculate.

I am happy, and completely at ease in his company, whereas with vainer men I am twitchy and distrustful.

What a peculiarly long and really rather painful journey this has proved to be. How much I have learned!

And already, this man is enhancing my life.

What The Children Think
29/6/2017

"Oh he looks so happy! What a fantastic smile! Oh I am in love! When can I meet them, when can I meet his son?" cries Faye, leaping up and down with excitement inside her car seat-belt, checking out Ben's picture on my phone, and a YouTube clip of his son singing an Ed Sheeran song, only looking and sounding considerably better than the original. "Have you kissed him yet?"

"Why've you got that badly applied fake tan?" queries Will.

"Well, actually, it isn't," I venture. "I seem to have met someone, and we've been outside a lot..."

"Oh good - I was worrying about you being all sad and alone as usual, in this beautiful weather," replies my beloved eighteen year old son.

- ends -

Printed in Great Britain
by Amazon